THE PARACEL ISLANDS AND
U.S. INTERESTS AND APPROACHES
IN THE SOUTH CHINA SEA

INTRODUCTION

As the People's Republic of China (PRC) rises in diplomatic, economic, and military stature in global politics, it is inexorably challenging the preeminent position that the United States of America has assumed since the demise of the Soviet Union. During this unprecedented rise, the relations between China and the United States may be conducted along a continuum of cooperation, competition, and conflict, making their many overlapping global interests complex, contested, and of crucial importance to the rest of the world. In one small area, however, their interactions are relatively simple and direct while remaining momentous and consequential, and thus their relations represent an interesting vantage point from which to analyze the actions between these two powers. Although the dispute over the Paracel Islands region in the South China Sea is between China and Vietnam, the United States has major interests there, and the dispute represents several global trends and problems affecting other states.

The Paracel Islands regional dispute is based on vital issues of territorial sovereignty, economic development, military security, and political legitimacy for Vietnam and China. For maritime and trading powers like India, Australia, the Republic of Korea (South Korea), Japan, and the United States, this local dispute holds significant worldwide consequences for use of the nautical domain concerning freedom of navigation and exploitation of the sea under maritime law, and for stability and prosperity along the world's busiest shipping lanes and one of its most rapidly expanding economic regions. The United States, as the de facto—if intermittent—guaranteer of stability and order in the world, has additional interests in maintaining an atmosphere in the Paracels in which diplomacy and the rule of international law address the dispute peacefully. In this way the Paracels are an illuminating study for larger problems like the nearby and more complicated dispute over the Spratly Islands. In comparison, the fewer participants and smaller area involved in the Paracels make this contest easier to study while still addressing issues of global importance and allowing discussions of potential parallel solutions on a smaller scale.

As a microcosm of the South China Sea disputes, this monograph delves into why the Paracel archipelago warrants examination by U.S. policymakers in order to discuss nuanced responses to the region's challenges. To attain that needed understanding, applicable legal aspects of customary and modern international laws are explored to analyze the competing maritime and territorial claims, and why and how Vietnam and China stake rival claims and opposing maritime legal rights. Throughout, the policies of the United States are examined through its conflicting interests in the region. Recommendations for how the United States should engage these issues, a more appropriate task than trying to solve the disputes outright, are then offered.

THE PARACEL ISLANDS REGION[1]
AND WHY IT IS IMPORTANT

The South China Sea is a body of water in Southeast Asia partially enclosed by the continental coasts of Vietnam and China, and portions of the shores of Taiwan, the Philippines, Malaysia, Brunei, and Indonesia. Hundreds of tiny geologic features dot the 122,648,000 square nautical miles (nm, or 1.5 times the size of the Mediterranean Sea) of the South China Sea. Its second largest natural grouping, the approximately 130^2 features of the Paracel Islands archipelago, covers about 2 square-nm of land above sea level spread across an area of about 13,000 square-nm of sea.[3] The Paracel Islands are located in the northwestern quarter of the South China Sea, centered approximately 185-nm east of the coast of Vietnam and 165-nm southeast of the Chinese island of Hainan Dao (see Map 1). These low coral islands consist of two main sub-chains: the Crescent Group to the west and the Amphitrite Group to the north, with additional isolated islands, reefs, and banks scattered further to sea (see Map 2). The Paracel Islands stretch 105-nm from northeastern Tree Island to southwestern Triton Island and 100-nm from northwestern North Reef to southeastern Herald Bank.[4] Around the Paracels, the ocean depth ranges from 1,000 to 2,000 meters (m), classifying it as part of the continental shelf of the Asian landmass and relatively shallow compared to the 3,000-m and deeper waters to the east and south. A finger of this deep water divides the Paracels in the north from mainland China and the eastern half of Hainan Dao.[5] Although unremarkable in its composition, the physical proximity and characteristics of these features, surrounding waters, and ocean floor play a very important role in the dispute over the Paracel Islands region and the potential ways to address this dispute.

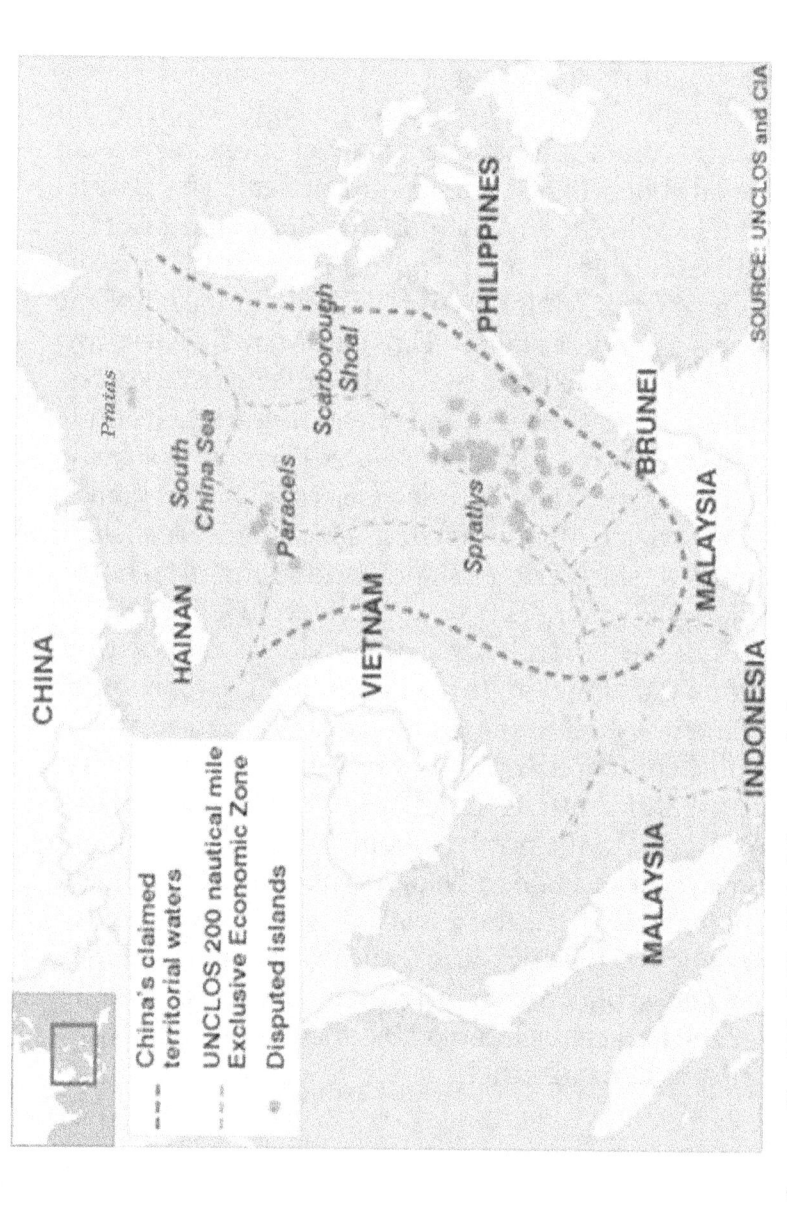

Source: David Lai, *The United States and China in Power Transition*, Carlisle, PA: Strategic Studies Institute, U.S. Army War College, December 2011.

Map 1. South China Sea.

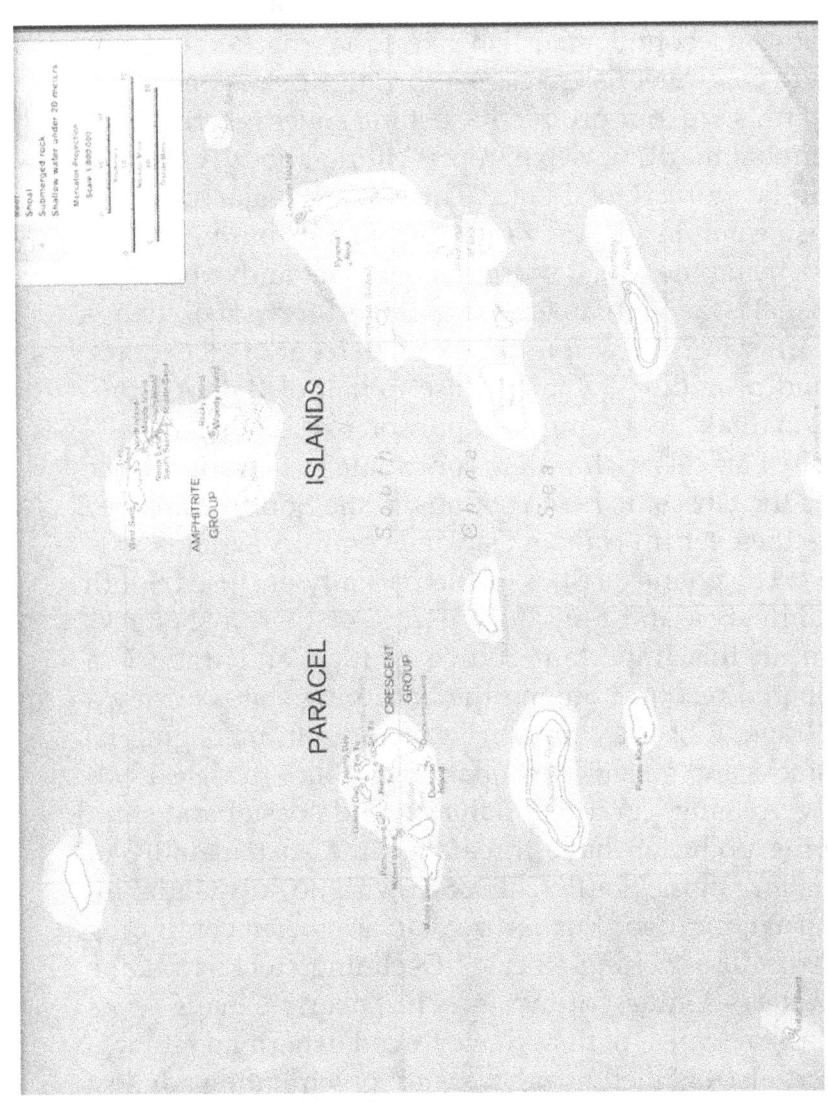

Source: Spratly Islands and Paracel Islands, Map 801947, Washington DC: CIA, April 1992.

Map 2. Paracel Islands.

Local Economic Importance of the Paracel Region.

Joining the Pacific and Indian Oceans, the warm South China Sea is among the most biologically diverse areas in the world, rich in both endangered species and commercial fish like tuna, mackerel, scads, and coral reef fish.[6] The South China Sea is one of the earth's top four productive fishing zones in terms of its annual maritime catch, representing about 10 percent of the world's total take.[7] This sea is a major source of fish eaten in Vietnam and China, contributing to China being the world's largest consumer and exporter of fish. It was Vietnam's second largest foreign exchange earner in 2010, accounting for 7 percent of all exports, and provides Vietnam "close to half of the total protein intake of a significant portion of the population."[8] The Paracels' rich waters contribute to this abundance as the closest fishing grounds in the South China Sea to the fleets in Hainan Dao and central Vietnam.[9]

The characteristics of the partially enclosed South China Sea and migratory nature of these fish stocks mean this important source of food and trade is a shared resource among the bordering states posing a "tragedy of the commons" dilemma in managing its stocks and genetic sustainability.[10] Since the late-1990s overfishing, coral reef damage, and coastal and shipping pollution have threatened the sustainability of fishing in the South China Sea with no substantial international coordination yet in place to halt continuing dwindling fishing stocks.[11] Declining stocks in home waters—China, for instance, has nearly exhausted its coastal waters of fish—have forced fisherman into waters also claimed by other states, precipitating adverse reactions by maritime law enforcement officials in order to protect the commercial interests within their claimed areas. Fishing-related incidents thus are common in the South China Sea and sometimes lead to diplomatic or armed clashes.[12]

The claiming of hydrocarbon energy resources in the South China Sea is another part of this maritime commons dispute. The South China Sea has been called a "second Persian Gulf" or "hydrocarbons Eldorado" for its rich potential,[13] leading some sources, like the Central Intelligence Agency's (CIA) *World Factbook*, to extrapolate the possibility for oil or natural gas strikes around the Paracel Islands.[14] However, the U.S. Energy Information Administration (USEIA) in 2013 gave virtually no proven or probable reserves for oil and less than .1 trillion cubic feet (tcf) for natural gas in the Paracel region. The USEIA's analysis of the underlying geology shows that most conventional hydrocarbon potential is located in the shallow coastal areas around the South China Sea and not in deeper waters like those surrounding the Paracel Islands, leaving in doubt the possibility for any economically recoverable conventional hydrocarbon finds there.[15] Although the Paracel region seems to lack other forms of hydrocarbon, initial tests promise significant amounts of methane hydrates,[16] a form of carbon energy considered more potent than coal, oil, and other types of natural gas. Due to technological limitations and the uncompetitive cost of extraction compared to conventional natural gas, methane hydrates are not recoverable economically at present, but represent "one of the world's largest reservoirs of carbon-based fuel" in the coming decades.[17] For both Vietnam and China, energy-starved but growing economies in societies imbued with long histories and cultures of patience, methane hydrates may be a future treasure trove if the oil and gas deposits found elsewhere in the South China Sea are not realized around the Paracel Islands.

Further afield in the South China Sea beyond the Paracel Islands, both Vietnam and China have exploited conventional oil and natural gas finds in their coastal areas — sometimes in direct contention with each other — by establishing capability for offshore drilling through international partners. Since the 1990s, Vietnam's national oil company, PetroVietnam, has expanded offshore oil and natural gas production through a variety of international companies including Chevron, British Petroleum (BP), ConocoPhillips, India's ONGC Videsh, Russia's Gazprom, ExxonMobil, and its current largest investor, the French independent Parenco.[18] Chevron is a partner in the Cuu Long and Phu Khanh Basins just offshore of southern Vietnam, exploiting fields estimated at 5-tcf in proven and probable reserves of natural gas, and BP helps develop the larger Nam Con Son centered 250-nm southeast of Ho Chi Minh City.[19]

China is the world's second largest consumer of energy, and its demand will double in the next 25 years, with more than half of that imported.[20] Since the early-1980s, China's largest national oil company, China National Offshore Oil Corporation (CNOOC), has been its main energy developer and principle partner with international companies like BP, Brazil's Petrobras, Petro-Canada, Australian BHP Billiton, and Hong Kong-owned and Canada-based Husky Energy. Initial Chinese offshore exploitation occurred in the nearby Pearl River Mouth Basin and the Qiongdongnan Basin (between Hainan Dao and the Paracels), but CNOOC has ventured into deeper water spurred by dwindling production. They discovered with Husky the Liwan 3-1 gas field about 200-nm southeast of Hong Kong, containing an estimated 4- to 6-tcf of proven or probable reserves of natural gas. CNOOC expects to produce .1-tcf annually from Liwan in 2014. They averaged 70 million barrels (bbl) of oil in 2011 from its other South China Sea operations. To expand its capability further, CNOOC launched its most advanced deep water drilling platform in 2011, costing $925 million, which first deployed in May 2014 as the Haiyang Shiyou 981 rig, 17 nm southwest of the Paracel's Triton Island, to explore in waters 120 nm from the Vietnamese coast on Vietnam's continental shelf.[21]

As the technical limits of drilling push further, the extensive overlapping claims by Vietnam and China in the South China Sea portend much competition and conflict between the two. For instance, in June 2012, rival territorial claims like the ones over the Jiangan and Wan'an Basins resulted in China unsuccessfully inviting foreign companies to explore nine drilling blocks approximately 60-nm east of Vietnam, drawing protests from Vietnam since PetroVietnam had already awarded these areas on its continental shelf to ExxonMobil and Gazprom for exploration. In 2012, Vietnam also protested China offering part of its Block 65, very close to the disputed Paracels, for development after unsuccessfully searching for a foreign company to engage in a nearby area in 2011.[22] About 200-nm southeast of Ho Chi Minh City, Vietnam drills energy from its Blue Dragon field "less than eight kilometers west of the [Chinese] Benton Block, and within or astride China's claim line," also exacerbating tensions between the two sides.[23] As of May 2014, tensions exploded when the Haiyang Shiyou 981 rig started exploring in waters 120 nm from the Vietnamese coast on Vietnam's continental shelf with an intense standoff between Vietnamese and Chinese maritime forces. Violence ensued with multiple at-sea collisions, the sinking of a Vietnamese fishing vessel, and anti-Chinese riots in Vietnam's cities that killed at least 4 people and were the worst in decades.[24]

Such conflicting operations also make doing other business in the region costly and risky, as demonstrated by Beijing's threats to foreign companies in China if they help develop the stakes of other claimants.[25] China also dominates the economy of Vietnam, which is vulnerable to Chinese pressure.[26] China disapproves of the more than 200 international companies contracted for oil and natural gas services by the coastal states in the greater South China Sea region because it internationalizes and complicates the dispute. In a *demarche* to Vietnam, China implied that only the companies of "claimant countries could be involved in such development activities," and made 18 such diplomatic protests between 2006 and 2007.[27] International energy companies have the expertise required to develop these waters but remain reluctant to do so without long-term stability in the region.[28] As one foreign energy analyst in Vietnam observed, "When push comes to shove, none of the foreign oil and gas companies are going to risk their business in China for something small in Vietnam."[29] The potential for major energy finds in the South China Sea has driven the surrounding states to press aggressive claims for this disputed commons, which in turn hobbles their efforts by making exploration and exploitation economically riskier, politically contentious, and militarily dangerous.

Unfortunately, the feuding South China Sea states "view the competition for access to and ownership of the resources as a zero-sum game."[30] For instance, after the 2008 dissolution of the disappointing Joint Maritime Seismic Undertaking (JMSU), the first and only multilateral cooperative arrangement among the

South China Sea states, its former members Vietnam, the Philippines, and the People's Republic of China (PRC) continued to explore unilaterally in their overlapping claimed areas, and China increased the number of its enforcement vessels in the region.[31] However, joint development in a contested area is not only possible, but can be mutually beneficial as demonstrated by Vietnam and Malaysia in a joint development area equidistant between their mainland coasts.[32] China has asserted it welcomes joint development activities in the South China Sea under the precondition that "sovereignty belongs to China," according to President Xi Jinping, echoing a policy strictly held since the 1980s.[33] China and Vietnam have subsequently agreed to a less involved joint exploratory agreement in the Gulf of Tonkin to which they expanded the region of interest to 2,500 square miles in 2013 and extended its duration to 2016.[34] Nonetheless, enforcement of territorial claims has intensified as new technology has made previously inaccessible offshore oil and gas more available, while high energy prices make their potential more lucrative.[35] Thus, political and armed clashes may occur in order to develop this energy potential before others exploit it first.

If the waters around the Paracels historically have been rich fishing grounds and today portend hydrocarbon wealth, the land features themselves have offered much less in economic activities and had not been permanently inhabited until the establishment of recent military garrisons.[36] The first visitors to the Paracels may have been Chinese traders collecting feathers and tortoise shells, but most of the early Chinese references to the South China Sea features mainly warned of the danger from the reefs, and the geologic features served mostly as landmarks to navigators and occasional shelter to fisherman.[37] During the 1920s, the Japanese trading company Mitsui Bussan Kaisha mined phosphates in the form of guano from Woody and Robert Islands, the Chinese government approved mining permits to its citizens into the 1940s, and the Republic of Vietnam (RVN or South Vietnam) awarded guano mining contracts in the Crescents in the 1950s and 1960s, but the latter were not economically viable.[38] The climate and tiny land area available in the Paracels offers little agricultural promise despite the rich guano deposits left by millennia of migratory ocean birds (there is no native terrestrial fauna except tortoises).[39] Some experts see the possibility for marine-based tourism in the region, and in April 2013, China authorized tourists to visit the Paracels.[40]

China, which currently controls the entire Paracel archipelago, is expanding tourism, fishing, and the military garrison on Woody Island, the archipelago's largest feature, as the foundations for a Paracels economy. To support its plans for ecotourism and other goals, the government plans to spend 10 billion yuan (U.S.$1.6 billion) on infrastructure improvements.[41] In addition to cruise boats and diving, the Chinese have organized other tourist and sporting activities such as a 2012 sailboat race to the disputed islands, despite objections from the Vietnamese government that such activities violate previous Chinese commitments not to "further complicate" the dispute over these territories.[42] However, all of this collecting, mining, and tourism potential of the islets financially pale in comparison to the surrounding waters' fishing and drilling activities. The islets have yet to produce any sustained economic yield, or as University of Helsinki Professor Timo Kivimaki concludes in his anthology on the South China Sea, "These areas have only been economically meaningful when the small reefs and islands have disrupted sea lines of communication."[43]

Regional Security Importance of the Paracels.

Although not economically consequential, the land features of the Paracels hold military importance for the states claiming them. The historically high amount of shipping that transits the South China Sea, the natural resource potential, and their strategic position from the coasts of southern China and central Vietnam give economic and security significance to the Paracel Islands.[44] China's primary defense interest in the South China Sea is to control its maritime "back door," as one Chinese scholar counted 479 attacks launched against China from the sea between 1840 and 1949, with 84 of those being major.[45] The Paracels have been a strategic position since the end of the Sino-French war in 1885 when France made Annam (central Vietnam) a protectorate, built a light house on the Paracel Islands, and began to press its claim for the islands.[46] As the Middle Kingdom, China had assumed its suzerainty over the South China Sea islands so that in 1876 China's ambassador to the United Kingdom (UK) specifically claimed the Paracels as Chinese territory, and in 1883 China terminated unauthorized German survey activities in the Paracels and Spratlys.[47] To reinforce its claims to the Paracels, imperial China landed a military survey team in 1907, annexed the islands in 1910, and tried to establish a presence in the area through military and scientific expeditions, but internal strife interfered with China establishing effective control.[48]

During the prelude to World War II, France formally claimed the Paracels in 1933 to counter the growing threat of imperial Japan to its Indochinese colonies, and set up a military weather station. By 1937, a French military report called a possible Japanese military presence in the Paracels intolerable for Indochina, with Britain urging the French to garrison the islands and build an airfield for their (and also British Malaya's) defense.[49] In 1938, French Vietnamese forces occupied the Paracels. Japan invaded the Paracels in turn in 1939, and annexed the islands by claiming to occupy the territory of China, with whom Japan was already at war.[50] Following World War II, Japanese forces withdrew from the Paracels in August 1945, and Republic of China (ROC or Taiwan after 1949) forces took control of the northern Amphitrite Group of the Paracels in October 1945 and occupied Woody Island in 1946. Meanwhile, the French made an unsuccessful attempt to force the ROC soldiers from the Paracels and settled for a foothold in the western Crescent Group by occupying Pattle Island with a platoon of Legionnaires.[51]

In 1950, the French government transferred responsibility for the defense of the Paracels to the Vietnamese.[52] Japan formally relinquished its claims to all of the South China Sea islands at the 1951 peace conference in San Francisco, but the conference members did not recognize China or Vietnam's claims to the islands.[53] The ROC forces withdrew from the Paracels during the Chinese Civil War, to be replaced by People's Liberation Army (PLA) troops in the mid-1950s, but during the gap between Chinese occupations, neither France nor Vietnam made an attempt to retake the vacated Amphitrite Group, opting instead to maintain good relations with China. The newly independent RVN took physical control of Pattle Island in 1954.[54] In February and March 1959, RVN forces challenged a slow infiltration of Chinese fisherman into the Crescent Group and subsequently occupied

Duncan, Drummond, and Palm Islands.[55] As each side became more focused on the Second Indochina War, the RVN withdrew from most of the Crescent Group in 1966, leaving only a civilian weather observation post on Pattle Island.[56]

After the 1973 Paris Peace Accords, American withdrawal from the region following its war in Vietnam, and discovery of oil deposits in the South China Sea, South Vietnam tried to reassert its position. China likely intended to slowly pressure the South Vietnamese from the Paracels, expecting the RVN government to crumble, and to take the islands from them and minimize potential objections from fellow communist rivals, the Soviet Union and Socialist Republic of Vietnam (SRV or North Vietnam), whose claim to them was conflicted.[57] In July and September 1973 the RVN announced contracts for exploring oil offshore, and re-declared its administration over the South China Sea islands.[58] In reply, on January 11, 1974, the PRC diplomatically challenged Vietnam's claims and for the first time linked its competing island claims with maritime rights.[59] In turn the RVN sent commandos, two cutters, one destroyer escort, and a mine sweeper to the Crescent Group, and on January 17, removed from Robert and Money Islands irregular forces deployed there by armed Chinese fishing vessels.[60] On January 19, RVN forces attempted to also take Duncan Island but were engaged by two PLA Navy (PLAN) sub-chasers and four mine sweepers that had rushed to the fighting and subsequently drove off the RVN forces. From that decisive 40-minute battle, probably one ship from each side was sunk, six ships severely damaged, 18 Chinese and 53 Vietnamese sailors killed, and 48 Vietnamese taken prisoner (including one American advisor). Although these results were incompletely reported and are questioned, the PRC indisputably controlled all of the Paracel Islands after the battle and remains its sole occupier.[61] For a century, the Paracels have been the prize for military forces controlling this strategic position in the South China Sea, and it remains militarily important today to its claimants.

After the Second Indochina War and reunification of Vietnam in 1975, hostility over territorial disputes continued between the two erstwhile communist allies, the PRC and the SRV. Minor military skirmishes continued around the Paracels into the 1990s, such as one in April 1979 in which China captured 24 Vietnamese troops, or March 1982, when Chinese forces held a Vietnamese reconnaissance boat and its crew of 10.[62] Another deadly naval clash occurred as China belatedly seized land features in the disputed Spratly Islands, also in the South China Sea. On March 14, 1988, warships from the PLAN and the Vietnam People's Navy (VPN) exchanged fire off Johnson Reef South, with the outgunned VPN losing around 70 sailors and up to three vessels, and the PLAN possibly losing one warship.[63] On March 19, 1992, the PLA landed on Da Ba Dau Reef, also in the Spratly Islands, resulting in a smaller skirmish with Vietnamese forces who already occupied nearby Sin Cowe East Island.[64] The most deadly example of the animosity between the SRV and the PRC, however, was a brief but ferocious land border war in 1979 in which Vietnam suffered between 35,000 and 62,000 casualties, and China suffered 20,000 to 63,500 casualties.[65] Although military forces between Vietnam and China have not clashed since the early-1990s this recent bloody history and other confrontations described further in this text make the situation dangerous for both these countries and for outside parties like the United States, who have interests in the region.[66]

With a history of foreign depredations—including the U.S. involvement in the Second Indochina War violating claimed Chinese and North Vietnamese sovereignty over the South China Sea—neither China nor Vietnam will tolerate foreigners taking advantage of their territory again.[67] This military legacy particularly menaces modern China's prosperity since 90 percent of its foreign trade was shipped, and 57 percent of petroleum and 27 percent of natural gas was imported from overseas in 2012, half of this energy imported through the South China Sea, destined for five of the world's top 10 busiest ports, which are Chinese.[68] To defend their national interests, Chinese military leaders consider the South China Sea important to the PRC's security. After examining China's many border disputes, Dr. M. Taylor Fravel, Chinese scholar at the Massachusetts Institute of Technology, concluded that "China has fought to protect its core interests including . . . the establishment of a maritime frontier."[69] Their maritime "near sea strategy" is to neutralize any threat within the "first island chain," defined as a line connecting Borneo, the Philippine, Taiwan, Ryukyu, Japanese, and Kurile Islands, to ensure access to the Pacific Ocean and prevent a "Great Wall in reverse."[70] Vietnamese Prime Minister Nguyen Tan Dung was also concerned about territorial disputes along key shipping lanes when he stated in 2013:

> A single irresponsible action or instigation of conflict could well lead to the interruption of such huge trade flow, thus causing unforeseeable consequences not only to regional economies, but also to the entire world.[71]

Such sentiment explains, in part, the regional contention for otherwise uninhabited and unproductive land features. Territorial disputes are the most common cause of fighting between states,[72] which is why one analyst dubbed the South China Sea islands "the least unlikely trigger" to start a conflict in the South China Sea.[73]

After gaining a foothold and then the entirety of the Paracel Islands, the PRC has administratively and militarily built them into its forward outpost in the South China Sea. The PLA began fortifying Woody Island in 1959, and since 1971 has steadily upgraded its facilities in the Paracels, including a military airfield begun in 1993 which is now a length of over 2,500-m.[74] This Woody Island facility allows operations of eight or more fourth generation Chinese fighter aircraft like the Su-30MKK or Su-27SK and the JH-7 bomber with combat ranges that could strike targets around the South China Sea, including Manila, the Philippines, and Ho Chi Minh City, Vietnam.[75] China also maintains two port facilties in the Paracels on Woody and Duncan Islands. The naval base on Woody Island is an artificial harbor with a concrete dock 500-m long and capable of accommodating destroyer and frigate class vessels.[76] The PLA also upgraded its South China Sea Sansha garrison to a division-level headquarters on Woody Island in 2012. Its responsibilities are "defense mobilization, . . . city [meaning municipal] guard, support for the city's disaster rescue and relief work, and [direction of] militia and reserve troops."[77] Actual defense of the Paracels, however, is given to the PLAN under the South Sea Fleet.[78] Some analysts see the increased military capabilities in the Paracels as an expansive move by the PRC in hard power, allowing it more influence in Southeast Asia and better control over its sovereign claims to the South China Sea, as well as acting as a potential platform to challenge U.S. power in the region.[79] In addition to the air and naval power projection capabilities the Paracels offer, the PRC has also turned them into a sophisticated signal and intelligence monitoring station that blankets some of the smaller satellite islands and is capable of monitoring nearly all of the South China Sea, including Vietnam, the Philippines, and high frequency signals from Malaysia.[80]

From its Paracel position, the PRC can control the busy South China Sea sea lanes and airspace militarily, and it may be the first strategic waypoint "pearl" in a power projection "necklace" that protects Chinese maritime interests and exerts influence from the South China Sea to the Persian Gulf.[81] From this perspective, Woody Island is "an unsinkable aircraft carrier" able to monitor and counter U.S. power in the region and deter its support to Taiwan or other nearby partners.[82] However, this view may alarmingly overstate the incremental military buildup that may be based simply on increased Chinese economic capacity and political interests. The establishment of a division-level headquarters, for instance, brings with it no additional troops and only reflects the Sansha municipality's administrative upgrade to "city" status.[83] Some commentators point out that military capabilities, like anti-ship missiles or strike aircraft, in the Paracels at best duplicate those already on Hainan Dao and thus add little new capability,[84] although basing on the Paracels does extend a weapon system's range by 175-nm into the South China Sea. The tiny Paracel Islands, however, do not allow basing of much significant military capability, and their forward position makes them vulnerable. As U.S. Rear Admiral (Retired) Mike McDevitt explained, "Putting garrisons on Woody Island or elsewhere in the Paracels would effectively maroon these guys, so the only advantage would be just showing the flag—to say, 'We are serious'."[85] Although militarily capable, the Paracels garrison may be as much a political declaration to better enforce sovereign and economic claims to the South China Sea as a military outpost.

The PRC, with its extensive claims and capable naval and maritime civilian forces, has been the most assertive in enforcing its claims in the South China Sea; however, Vietnam and other bordering states have also emphasized their claimed rights in the region, using naval forces against other states' perceived encroaching commercial activities. For example, from February and March 1959, South Vietnam used its naval advantage to evict Chinese fisherman from Duncan Island and finally gained firm control of the Crescent Group.[86] In return, China began naval patrols around the Paracels in 1960 and extended them throughout most of the South China Sea by 1987, boldly protecting an area that it considers its "inherent territories."[87] The Chinese believe they are defending their waters against "increasing encroachment on the part of Vietnam, and the Philippines in particular, and what they [the Chinese] saw as self-serving meddling by the U.S."[88] Patrolling by both Vietnam and China has resulted in cycles of aggression by naval ships against foreign civil vessels, leading to numerous illegal actions cited against the other side's navy.[89] Such incidents peaked in number and intensity of violence between 1987 and 1995. Although less frequent now, a recent example occurred in May 2011 when PLAN vessels used weapons to threaten Vietnamese fisherman in disputed South China Sea waters, and in June when the VPN carried out live fire exercises as part of a larger protest against Chinese actions.[90] Naval ships from all of the states have, nonetheless, played a more subdued role in these waters, despite the occasional threat or use of armed naval vessels to counter foreign violations.[91]

Instead of its navy, China now prefers to use its maritime law enforcement ships to protect its claims, although backed by the PLAN which often shadows just over the horizon.[92] Five disparate PRC maritime enforcement agencies have aggressively policed China's interests and kept tensions high throughout the South China Sea.[93] In 2013, the Chinese government consolidated four of these agencies into a single paramilitary coast guard called China Marine Surveillance under a new National Oceanic Administration, creating an "'iron fist' that would replace ineffective operations scattered among a number of agencies."[94] This streamlining may only partially rein in the aggressive nature of Chinese patrolling, since other ministries within China have conflicting views on the South China Sea disputes with the "policy of reactive assertiveness, characterised by strong reactions to provocations by other parties" still practiced after the reorganization.[95] Whereas before the consolidation only one of these agencies was armed, under the new coast guard, all of the vessels will be armed, and the number of sailors and vessels will increase significantly.[96]

This buildup is meant to counter foreign violations into China's claimed waters. China reported 1,303 foreign ships and 214 foreign aircraft "intrusions" into its claimed space in 2010, an increase from a total of 110 intrusions in 2007.[97] In 2009, the PRC's South Sea Region Fisheries Administration Bureau (SSRFAB) detained 33 Vietnamese ships and seven more in 2010.[98] In May 2011, the Vietnamese claim that a Chinese enforcement ship cut the cables of a PetroVietnam oil and gas survey ship in disputed waters near Vietnam, and in June, a Chinese fishing vessel intentionally rammed the exploration cables of another Vietnamese survey ship.[99] Well-reported incidents in 2013 include a Vietnamese trawler damaged by flares fired from a Chinese vessel near the Paracel Islands in March, the ramming and damaging of a Vietnamese fishing boat off the coast of Vietnam in June, and the beating of fisherman and eviction of two Vietnamese fishing boats by the Chinese in Paracels waters in July.[100]

Some of these incidents have been attributed to Chinese fishing vessels acting as an auxiliary to enforcement agencies as demonstrated in the 2012 Scarborough Shoal standoff between vessels from China and the Philippines in the South China Sea.[101] Although events involving naval vessels have subsided, the level of police and commercial vessel incidents has increased as a result of China's tripling its patrols at sea since 2008. These pose different but serious problems because civilian vessels have been "easier to deploy, operate under looser chains of command, and engage more readily in skirmishes."[102] The U.S. Pacific Fleet Deputy Chief of Staff for Intelligence and Information, speaking at a conference in a personal capacity recently, warned that the PLAN is using its civilian proxies for "maritime confrontations [that] haven't been happening close to the Chinese mainland. Rather, China is negotiating for control of other nations' resources off their coasts."[103] Stephanie Kleine-Ahlbrandt, head of the Beijing office of the International Crisis Group, called it "a brilliant strategy by China to establish their control over an area without firing a single shot."[104] PRC vessels have been active in enforcing China's maritime claims in the South China Sea, exacerbating the tensions among the states involved, as demonstrated by the Haiyang Shiyou 981 clashes near Triton Island.

All of the claimants in the Spratly and Paracel Islands disputes have also reacted with force against Chinese commercial vessels.[105] Since 1989, more than 300 incidents against Chinese trawlers have been reported including being fired upon, seized, or expelled, with three fishermen wounded and 10 ships detained by the Vietnamese in 2010 alone.[106] Throughout the South China Sea, China's data shows 750 of its fishing vessels were robbed, seized, or attacked between 1989 and 2010, with 25 fishermen killed or missing, 24 injured, and 800 arrested from waters China claims as its own. Despite the lucrative return from fishing in the Paracels region, Chinese fishermen are reluctant to fish these waters for fear of being attacked or arrested by Vietnamese marine authorities.[107] As the relative lull in naval and police actions in the South China Sea during the 2000s seems to be ending, some analysts fear that a major discovery of energy resources could fan the flames of more serious clashes in a region lacking the mechanisms for conflict management.[108] The International Crisis Group observes, "While the likelihood of major conflict remains low, all of the trends are in the wrong direction, and prospects of resolution are diminishing."[109] Those assessments bode poorly for the region's states and for the United States, which also has significant interests there.

Importance of the Paracels Region to the United States.

In addition to the South China Sea region holding huge potential for producing oil and natural gas, it is also one of the world's great thoroughfares of energy and trade, adding to its strategic significance to the United States and the international community.[110] The United Nations (UN) Conference on Trade and Development estimated that 8.4 million tons of maritime trade—more than half of the world's annual total—passed into the South China Sea in 2010. The USEIA estimates that around 6-tcf of natural gas—over half of the world's maritime gas movement—was part of that trade, as was approximately 14 trillion barrels of oil, or a third of the world's volume. These massive movements link energy-rich southwest Asia and northern Africa to economically vibrant northeast Asia.[111] An estimated 80 percent of Taiwanese, 66 percent of South Korean, and 60 percent of Japanese energy supplies are imported via the South China Sea, which also accounts for 40 percent of Japan's total exports and imports.[112] These busiest shipping lanes in the world pass by the strategically placed Paracel Islands, [113] and the sea lanes' security is crucial to nearby states with which the United States has a range of formal defense arrangements, including Taiwan, South Korea, Japan, Australia, the Philippines, Thailand, and Singapore.[114] Economic development in East Asia and the world would be seriously set back should maritime trade in the South China Sea be disrupted.[115] The PRC, ROC, and Vietnam each claim all of the Paracel Islands and most of the South China Sea, and these conflicting and extensive maritime claims also challenge U.S. economic interests to exploit water column and seabed resources on what many parties consider high seas or international waters.[116] U.S. economic interests are directly and indirectly entwined in the competition over the distant Paracel Islands.

As this monograph has shown, this region is not just another global hot spot, but one with important long-term economic, territorial, and security contentions. It is not only one of the world's most disputed ocean areas, but also one of the few where violent incidents routinely occur at sea.[117] For diplomatic, historic, and military capacity reasons, other states in and around the region rely on the United States to ensure stability in the South China Sea.[118] This dependence could make the South China Sea a convenient arena for a rising China to test U.S. political will and dominance through increasingly assertive incidents to which the United States must respond to protect partner and American security and economic interests.[119] A senior fellow at the Atlantic Council observed that "some in China may have believed that the global financial crisis that started in late-2007 signaled a U.S. decline of the U.S. and that the time was ripe to become more assertive."[120] Thus, the United States may face the difficult dilemma of balancing its interests in support of allies and partners with protecting its political and economic relations with the PRC.[121] For these reasons, the American journalist and Stratfor analysis Robert Kaplan dubbed the South China Sea the world's "new central theater of conflict" and "the heart of political geography in coming decades."[122]

Yet mutual economic and political interdependence among these states — and the United States — argues against major conflict or even a Cold War style rivalry.[123] Each state with interests in the South China Sea also understands the cooperative need for stability, sustainable management of resources, freedom of navigation, crime prevention, and a host of other common interests in the region which cannot be attained alone or by force.[124] Indeed, in 1998, the United States and PRC signed the "Establishing a Consultation Mechanism to Strengthen Military Maritime Safety (or the Military Maritime Consultative Agreement [MMCA])," designed to prevent incidents between them.[125] Nonetheless, concerns remain that strong motivations, existing tensions, and entrenched positions need only an accident or miscommunication to create an incident or open conflict that subjugates all of these interests.[126] Another reason why the South China Sea is important to the United States is that such incidents already occur.

Although ostensibly neutral and not a part of any of the land or maritime claims in the South China Sea, the United States and other seafaring states do have international rights in the area which have been challenged in contentious ways—the basis for which are explained in the next section.[127] The comprehensive claims by the PRC to all of the waters of the South China Sea, and its government's interpretation of international law, encourage the Chinese to bar any activity by foreign military vessels and aircraft from what most other states determine to be high seas and "transitable" Chinese maritime jurisdictions.[128] Some analysts believe that U.S. surveillance actions in the northern South China Sea, which China contends trespasses on its jurisdiction, risk drawing the United States into a conflict in the region.[129] Although this concern is now based on events in proximity of Chinese mainland waters, China has protested U.S. patrols around the Paracel archipelago since the 1960s.[130] Should the PRC prevail in its claims to land features and waters around the Spratly and Paracel Islands, the entire South China Sea could become a Chinese lake off-limits to foreign government vessels without permission.

Despite the deconfliction efforts of the 1998 MMCA, aggressive incidents have occurred between

Chinese vessels and U.S. craft exercising freedom of navigation rights. Some of these may have been deliberate clashes by Chinese commercial vessels to create an incident and show the damaging effects of military activities in exclusive economic zones (EEZs).[131] The most serious military-to-military incident was the 2001 collision of a Chinese fighter jet with a U.S. Navy EP-3 65 miles southeast of Hainan Dao, which killed the Chinese pilot and forced the American crew to an emergency landing at the Chinese base on Hainan Dao.[132] On the surface, Chinese vessels have harassed the U.S. ocean surveillance fleet ships, including the USNS *Bowditch* (2001 and 2002), *Bruce C. Heezen* (2003), *Victorious* (2003 and 2004), *Effective* (2004), *John McDonnell* (2005), *Mary Sears* (2005), *Loyal* (2005), and *Impeccable* (2009).[133] During this last incident, five Chinese vessels surrounded the hydrographic survey ship roughly 75 miles southeast of Hainan Dao (half way to the Paracels) and attempted to snag its towing cable, to which the U.S. Navy responded by dispatching warships to escort subsequent unarmed survey and ocean surveillance vessels.[134] However, in December 2013 a renewed round of tensions started with the PRC establishing an air defense identification zone (ADIZ) over disputed islands in the East China Sea with the establishment of a similar ADIZ possible in the South China Sea, and a near-collision incident between the USS *Cowpens* and escort vessels of the PRC's *Liaoning* carrier battle group in disputed international waters of the South China Sea.[135] Even if the United States held absolute neutrality among the disputants, it might still be drawn into the South China Sea fracas to reinforce its maritime rights guaranteed under international law.

LEGAL BASIS AND CLAIMS IN THE PARACEL ISLANDS DISPUTE

What is the cause of this melee over land sovereignty, maritime jurisdiction, assertion of international rights, and police and military incidents around the South China Sea? To best understand the issues and in order to better contribute to their solution, this section analyzes the customary (or traditional) law which governs disputes over sovereignty of land and some forms of maritime jurisdiction and rights, and the 1982 *United Nations Convention on the Law of the Sea* (UNCLOS, or Law of the Sea Treaty) which only addresses maritime issues, but in a more comprehensive and coherent manner.[136] This section also examines how each of the involved parties applies these concepts to support these contentious claims. In this section, disputes over land sovereignty generally are treated distinctly from maritime jurisdiction disputes, although either claim may depend upon the legal standing of the other and may blur together in the case of historic rights claims, as will be shown.[137] Sovereignty determination over geologic features, boundary delimitation of maritime borders, and the nature of those features as productive islands or uninhabitable rocks are three crucial decisions for which the claimants contest.[138] Concepts here are covered to the depth needed to apply to the South China Sea and are not meant to be comprehensive. Complicating such an examination are the facts that international law is neither complete nor rigorous enough to be "a constitution" to consider the full merit of competing claims,[139] and some modern legal regimes may conflict with customary precepts.[140] Thus, legal applications may not be the ultimate arbiter to resolve the many differences, but knowing the basis of these legal claims may better guide potential ways to manage disputes.[141] In large part, these legal disputes are how the contenders present their claims, so examining them this way is useful to illustrate the issues involved.

Customary International Laws and Claims.

Although by themselves the land features of the Paracel Islands have sustained no human population and produced little economically, they are points of contention because an island may garner legal jurisdiction and control over adjoining waters and resources.[142] To establish these benefits, a state uses customary, or traditional, international law to stake its claim through long association in a historic claim or discovery and occupation of a feature—each is a separate mechanism to establish sovereignty, but some states employ them together like overlapping insurance policies. Once sovereignty is determined, the type of feature owned dictates the forms of maritime jurisdictions that then extend from it.[143]

Like common law, customary law has evolved over the centuries mainly from European traditions based on generally accepted notions, or past precedence through agreements, arbitration, or rulings by international courts. Concepts in customary law evolve as state practices change, and tend to address only specific issues presented within certain contexts. Among Asian societies, Western customary legal concepts like sovereignty, the high seas, or coastal jurisdiction have no traditional equivalent which makes adjudicating ancient claims incongruent with modern procedures.[144] The SRV and PRC, as socialist governments, also assert that "bourgeois international law serves the interests of the bourgeoisie only," although each employs these methods to advance their interests even as they seek to change them.[145] Customary law is also not codified and agreed upon in as rigorous a manner as UNCLOS. All of this makes traditional law exceedingly complex and open to many interpretations and differences in its application.[146]

UNCLOS purposefully does not address sovereignty over land and "is premised on the assumption that a particular state has undisputed title over territory from which the maritime zone is claimed."[147] Thus customary law is the usual means to settle sovereignty disputes over territory through international law (though other means exist like conquest or purchase), and its maritime customs are still sometimes invoked today. UNCLOS indirectly has spurred island claims since its negotiations began in the 1970s by assigning oceanic jurisdiction to nearly any land feature, thereby converting previously avoided desolate rocky obstacles into the focal points of potential oceanic riches and igniting a form of gold rush over the South China Sea islets. Along with new technologies and rapidly expanding populations and economic needs, the new Law of the Sea Treaty explains why island disputes have turned more serious and violent in the South China Sea since the 1970s, and why we study old legal principles to understand a 21st century problem.[148]

Historic Vietnamese and Chinese Claims under Customary Law.

The oldest method of establishing jurisdiction over the features and waters of the South China Sea is to claim "historic rights," "historic waters," or "historic title" to them. In essence, this concept states that an area has been part of a state, through long continuous administrative control, economic use, or social links, should give the claimant special consideration. Such consideration could include inherent usage rights in the area, or control over it as internal waters or sovereign territory when the claim is generally recognized by other states.[149] The appeal of maintaining a doctrine of historic claims comes from the legal principle of *stare decisis* ("maintain what has been decided," or settled law) offering the advantage of stability and continuity in law and governance, which is why it was accepted as a precept by the International Court of Justice (ICJ) in 1951.[150] In contrast, in traditional East Asian politics before Western legal concepts were practiced, the historic association of a region to a people or state would not need a formal legal claim to perennially oversee or control it.[151]

Although a practical customary precept, historic claims are broad and not well defined traditionally or in the Law of the Sea Treaty, even in Western international law.[152] Generally, historic rights recognize that traditional activities may continue in a designated area, and, if specifically stated, may include a claim to a land area or maritime jurisdiction.[153] The concept of historic claims, "over which a nation exercises sovereign authority," has been occasionally noted "under international law in limited situations," but the ambiguity of these concepts' wide-ranging and sometimes conflicting interpretations means they may not be useful mechanisms for establishing control.[154] Nonetheless, when such claims are made, they are accompanied by detailed historic documentation to build a case in favor of the claimant, which would then need to be verified and weighed against other conflicting claims. Such procedures favor cultures with long traditions in writing and recordkeeping. Using this mechanism to establish sovereignty or jurisdiction under modern practices requires that claims be backed by effective, continuous, and unchallenged occupation or administration in order to be valid.[155] These latter criteria are usually hard to establish, and thus may account in part for the past and present practice of challenging or ejecting noncitizens from disputed areas in order to demonstrate some control over the claims,[156] resulting in some of the violent incidents this monograph has documented.

The South China Sea region has conflicting historic claims made by China and Vietnam.[157] Vietnam presents a classic historic case for all of the Spratly and Paracel Islands and an undelimitated amount of much of the South China Sea based on four historical arguments presented in three White Papers in 1979, 1982, and 1988.[158] As evidence, Vietnam presents historic records and maps, physical geographic data, and references to stele inscribed in Vietnamese showing it controlled and exploited the Paracels by citing court documents from as early as the reign of King Le Tanh Tong (1460-97).[159] They also cite corroborating European missionaries, navigators, and geographers of that time, and references in the Dutch *Journal of Batavia* from the 1630s supporting their claims to the Paracels.[160] Stronger proof from royal court sources are dated from 1802 when the Nguyen Dynasty (1802-1945) pursued a more active maritime policy through "systematic measures taken in the fields of administration, defense, transport, and economic exploitation."[161] Such evidence bolsters the Vietnamese claim "that the 'Feudal Vietnamese State' effectively controlled the two archipelagoes since the 17th century according to international law."[162] Vietnam also invokes the 1884 French claim and administration over the Paracels while the Vietnamese states were a French protectorate and ultimate successor to their Western legal-style claim.[163] From such proof, a modern Vietnamese scholar could assert that "a long time ago, regional countries pursued their normal activities in the East Sea without encountering any Chinese impediment and they have never recognized China's historic rights in the South China Sea. . . ."[164] More archival records are being translated into English to bolster Vietnam's historic claim to the entire region.[165]

The Vietnamese historic claim to the Paracel Islands tends to be inconclusive, however. Many non-Vietnamese scholars have found that basic Vietnamese knowledge about the South China Sea region in its historic documents was weak and depended heavily on misperceptions of the region conveyed by Europeans. As more accurate information about the Paracels was attained by Vietnamese authorities during the 19th century, "there is little evidence that the Nguyen dynasty upheld its claim through declarations, effective occupation, or utilization."[166] The Vietnamese claim has not been generally recognized, having been ignored in the 1951 peace conference in San Francisco, CA, in which Japan relinquished control of the islands after World War II. Additionally, Vietnam's claim has been consistently protested and interfered with by China since the 1900s.[167] Other telling blows were official statements by the Democratic Republic of Vietnam's (North Vietnam)[168] Second Foreign Minister in 1956 and Prime Minister in 1958 that recognized the PRC's stated territorial claims, which included both the Paracel and Spratly Islands, even while acknowledging disagreements over their land border.[169] In 1958, the transfer from China to North Vietnam of the disputed White Dragon Tail Island, a speck in the Gulf of Tonkin, was possibly a *quid pro quo* for recognition of China's control over the South China Sea islands.[170] Not surprisingly, the Hanoi government offered no protest when the PLAN defeated the RVN Navy in 1974, and the PRC occupied the entire Paracels group. That same government today renounces its earlier support to PRC territorial claims as a necessity during its wars against foreigners,[171] but such recent recantations only underscore a weak historic claim as difficult to support.

The Chinese historic claim to the South China Sea and its geologic features is even more extensive than the Vietnamese stake,[172] but just as ill-defined. Whether China claims all of the sea and resources of the region (as indicated in terms officially used like "territorial waters"), just the land features within the South China Sea (as may be intended with assertions to a "historic title"), unspecified traditional rights in the region, like fishing, or some combination of these, they are voraciously defended as "historically belonging to China" and "China's intrinsic and inseparable territories" under the historic claim doctrine.[173] Such ambiguity has been consistent and probably purposeful by both Chinese governments, since it allows flexibility on the Chinese side to argue conflicting points in its various maritime disputes and has made negotiations for the other claimants more difficult.[174] Further complicating matters is that both the PRC and ROC assert identical historic and other claims to the South China Sea based on the same evidence. This mutual position could be termed "China's" or the "Chinese" claim, terms which this analysis employs as pertaining to both or to any pre-1949 Chinese government.[175] Since both sides recognize only one China, to support a lesser claim than the one already made could weaken that government's appearance of legitimacy—a phenomenon making settling of disputes in the South China Sea more difficult.[176] Although the claims are the same for both, the Taiwanese government has rarely asserted them as boldly or physically as has the PRC.[177] Since, unlike the PRC and Vietnam, the ROC has no foothold or proximity to the Paracel Islands, its coverage in this monograph generally refers to its actions before 1949, and is otherwise assumed to support the PRC's position in the South China Sea disputes.

The Chinese assert their ancient use of the sea through archeological evidence of fishing and trading activities, naval expeditions during the Han (206 BC-220 AD) and Ming (1368-1644) Dynasties, and development of a "Marine Silk Route" to Arabia and Africa during the Tang (618-907) and Song (960-1279) Dynasties.[178] The first written records cited to support a historic claim include an indirect reference to the islands in 1178, and the *Chu Fan Chi* (*A Description of Barbarous People*) written between 1225 and 1242 by an imperial foreign trade inspector, Chau Ju-kau, in which he refers to "long sand banks in the islands" thought to mean the Paracels, and recorded the Paracels within the border of China in 1279.[179] Chinese association with the Paracels is better documented from the late-1800s through diplomatic interactions with European powers when, for instance, in 1876, China's ambassador to Great Britain declared the Paracel Islands Chinese territory; in 1877, when China and France completed an ill-defined maritime boundary agreement in the Gulf of Tonkin; and in 1883, when the Chinese expelled a German survey team from the Paracel Islands.[180] A Chinese survey in 1928 delimited the Paracel Islands as China's southern border, but did not include the more southerly Spratly Islands.[181] To clarify its heretofore inconsistent claims against other powers in the South China Sea, in 1935, a Chinese committee on land and water boundaries published a list specifying 28 Paracel and 96 Spratly land features above low tide level as Chinese territory.[182] Over the past 2,000 years, the Chinese avow to be the first to discover, name, and administer the South China Sea islands.[183]

In 1947, the ROC consolidated the Chinese historic claim by publishing a map with its "traditional maritime boundary line" (more often referred to as the "9-dashed line," "U-shaped line," or the "cow's tongue" [see Map 1]) enclosing most of the South China Sea waters and associated land features as its "indisputable sovereignty."[184] The Chinese claim their historic links to the Paracels were well recognized until the 1930s when the French made claim to them through their then colonial possession of Vietnam, and the Japanese annexed the Paracels during World War II. In their support, the Chinese cite an 1887 Sino-French treaty in which all islands east of a delimitation line belonged to China. Both the Spratly and Paracel Islands lie east of this line, although neither was specifically named, and the French would later contest that the treaty was a local agreement and not one of such wide scope.[185] Nonetheless, during the prelude to World War II, the Chinese claim that the French assured them that its "garrison in the Paracels had a defensive purpose and would not prejudice the legal resolution of the dispute."[186] The ROC's 1947 claims were echoed by the PRC when it claimed sovereignty over the Paracel and Spratly Islands in 1951 and over maritime rights from these features in 1958. These claims were formally reiterated in PRC law in 1992 and 1998, and diplomatically in 2009 when China submitted its 9-line claim to UNCLOS.[187] Taiwan codified its historic waters claim to the region within its U-shaped line in 1993 in its *South China Sea Policy Guidelines*, and reemphasized its broad claim as recently as 2011.[188] Thus the Chinese historic claim to the region has been reinforced in domestic law and recent proclamation by both the PRC and ROC.

Despite this historic documentation claiming the Paracels and the South China Sea, there are problems with Chinese arguments because its association has often lacked the clear consistent claims or effective administration required by modern international judgments.[189] Although it suffers from the same flaws, Vietnam's historic claim contests China's assertions to acquiescence by other states and that it has been a victim of European imperial aggression. Vietnam, for instance, refuses to stamp new PRC passports bearing a map showing the South China Sea as part of China, and has opposed an annual May-to-August fishing ban in the South China Sea imposed by China.[190] Non-Chinese scholars also note that competing claims for some or all of the Paracel Islands have been made since the 1800s by France and Japan, pushing China into asserting formal Western legal style sovereignty claims.[191] China's counterarguments that its sovereignty over the Paracels was strong until French incursions in the 1930s are viewed dimly in light of inconsistent claims and the weak exercise of authority up to the end of World War II.[192] During the 1943 Cairo Conference among the belligerents fighting Japan, attending ROC President Chiang Kai-shek made no claims for any Japanese occupied territory in the Paracels or Spratlys, despite the fact that decisions about occupied lands was a main topic of the conference. Also, during the 1951 negotiations over the peace treaty with Japan, 47 of 50 participating countries rejected a Soviet call to assign the Japanese-conquered areas, including the Spratlys and Paracels, to the PRC.[193] A senior intelligence officer at the U.S. Pacific Fleet in a personal capacity at the U.S. Naval Institute challenged Chinese historic claims further when he declared in 2013 that:

> the rubric of a maritime history that is not only contested in the international community but has largely been fabricated by Chinese government propaganda bureaus in order to . . . 'educate' the populace about China's rich maritime history.[194]

Chinese and Vietnamese officials have shown historic use of the South China Sea and its features but not to the level needed to establish effective and continuous control and sovereignty, since other states were also using and claiming parts of this area during these periods.[195] Some commentators believe China and Vietnam might have more success by converting their historic sovereignty claims to one of historic rights to things like fishing, a better documented historic activity by both in the region.[196] In short, the Chinese and Vietnamese historic claims for control over the Paracel Islands and their surrounding waters "can generally be summarized as incomplete, intermittent, and unconvincing."[197] Widely accepted international precedents, like the Island of Palmas Case ruled by the Permanent Court of Arbitration in 1925 and in subsequent cases,[198] find effective administration and occupation of land take precedence over first discovery, historic claims, or close proximity.[199] The Vietnamese and Chinese historic claims to the Paracel Islands lack a sufficient weight of evidence to establish the requirements of a sustainable population, persistent effective control by the respective governments, or of enduring economic activity to establish clear sovereignty.[200]

*Sovereign Claims under the Customary Law
of Discovery and Occupation.*

More in accord with modern customary legal precepts—because it is centered on effective control—is the customary legal principle of discovery and occupation. China and Vietnam each staked out some of the Paracel Islands using this method, but since the 1974 Battle of the Paracels, only China physically occupies the archipelago. Like historic claims, which are increasingly being held to the same modern standard of effective administration, land stakes made through discovery and occupation require that a claim first be made for a land feature and then consistently and effectively controlled to remain valid.[201] This land must previously be *res nullis* ("nobody's property"),[202] and thus "discovered," and open for occupation and exploitation. More important is the "subsequent continuous and effective acts of occupation, generally construed to mean permanent settlement," although for uninhabitable islands that standard may be less strict but then garners fewer jurisdictional rights, as will be covered in the next section.[203] Using the indeterminate nature of historic claim law, one could argue that historic claims fall under the doctrine of discovery and occupation through long-term association, although the difference in evidence presented, time frames, and inclusion of historic waters or rights may make them separate types of claims, which are often how the parties to the disputes present them.

In the South China Sea, formal discovery and occupation claims started in the 1800s. However, the Philippines government, for one, insists that, when defeated Japan renounced its World War II annexations, it left a void in ownership, arguably resetting all the geologic features in the South China Sea to *res nullis*.[204] Vietnam's history occupying the Paracels was presented earlier in this monograph. Since Vietnam currently has no physical control of this island group, its occupation claims are anemic, although the government still acts in ways consistent with administering the Paracels. The Chinese discovery and occupation claim is examined in this section in terms of the evolving requirements for effective control and habitation, which account for the recent interest over the past 50 years in occupying the land features of the Paracel and Spratly Islands (mainly through military garrisons so far) from which they would then seek to establish improved sovereignty over the islets and their surrounding seas.[205]

In addition to—and supporting—its historic claim, China also asserts that "Beijing has indisputable sovereignty over the islands based on discovery and prior occupation" as PRC President Yan Shang Kun declared in 1991.[206] Under its modern application, discovery and occupation of the Paracel Islands began in 1946 after ROC President Chiang Kai-shek ordered the occupation of the Amphitrite Group and followed this with the publication of the infamous U-shaped line claim to the South China Sea.[207] Despite the fact that Nationalist China withdrew its forces in May 1950 after its defeat in the Chinese Civil War, the ROC continued to assert its claim over the archipelago based on the 1952 Sino-Japanese Treaty which recognized Chinese sovereignty over the Paracels. However, Japan had previously renounced all claims to the South China Sea islands with no successor assigned, and the 1951 San Francisco Treaty refused to recognize any Paracels claims. Undeterred, the ROC government retorted that such actions could not nullify Chinese sovereignty grounded on earlier historic claims and occupation.[208]

Bracketing the ROC's initial occupation was the PRC's subsequent occupation of the Amphitrites in 1956 when it established a physical PLA presence in the archipelago, allowing the PRC to control it all since 1974. This Chinese claim received an unintended boost in 1939 when imperial Japan dismissed French protests of its invasion of the Paracels, countering that they were Chinese and not French possessions.[209] The Chinese occupation also was complemented by an earlier legal claim to all of the Paracels by the PRC in 1951, and to maritime rights from these features in 1958.[210] As noted earlier, PRC occupation claims were strengthened by proclamations in 1956 and 1958 by DRV officials acknowledging the PRC claims to the South China Sea islands, and with Vietnam possibly acquiring White Dragon Tail Island in return.[211] After oil was discovered in the South China Sea, the PRC strengthened its only foothold in the region, the Amphitrites, by improving infrastructure there, and in January 1974 sought to extend its physical control over all of the Paracels when it sent armed citizens to vacant RVN-claimed Robert, Money, Duncan, and Drummond Islands to build shelters and show the Chinese flag. This precipitated the Battle of the Paracels and full PRC control of the archipelago.[212] Administrative control was consolidated under PRC laws passed in 1992 and 1998, specifying Chinese maritime jurisdiction and rights.[213] China has since improved infrastructure and living conditions on Woody Island and adjoining Rocky Island, including roads and a causeway, government and military buildings, a hospital, a hostel, a post office, and commercial shops.[214] China furthered its administrative control in July 2012 with the promotion of Sansha City, headquartered on Woody Island, as the administrative prefecture-level city for all of its South China Sea claims including the Paracel and Spratly Islands.[215] These actions by China are meant to show "effective occupation" of the Paracel Islands, and may with time "ripen into a legitimate assertion of sovereignty." In this way, China is adhering to modern international legal practices.[216]

Just as the Chinese historic claim has been contested, so, too, has its discovery and occupation claims, though with much less effect since 1974. After World War II, France sent an expedition to the Spratlys to dislodge the Chinese occupation and reestablish its claims by leaving a physical presence in the Crescents.[217] While still occupied by both South Vietnam and the PRC in 1973, the Saigon government actively explored for oil around the Paracels and Spratlys with Western oil companies and incorporated the islands into Vietnamese provinces, directly challenging Chinese claims and setting the stage for the naval battle in the following year.[218] Despite losing physical control of the Paracels, the SRV has continued actions to administer it by incorporating it as an island district in the Da Nang independent municipality and subjecting it to Vietnamese laws.[219] As recently as June 2012, Vietnam passed a maritime law reasserting its sovereignty over the Paracel and Spratly Islands and delimiting its maritime claims for both.[220] On the same day, in response to this challenge to its claimed sovereignty, China upgraded the status of Sansha City. Vietnam and the Philippines expectedly protested but, unusually, so did the United States.[221] China's claims to the Paracels have been contested by other states, although its current extended occupation is harder to counter.

With Vietnam's historic South China Sea claims no stronger than China's, it has relied on physical occupation of some of the islets in the Spratly Islands to reinforce its claims. However, this practice severely undercuts Vietnam's own discovery and occupation claim in the China-dominated Paracel Islands.[222] Vietnam has documented its occupation of the Paracels back to 1816, with the Jialong Dynasty emperor ordering construction of temples and monuments on the islands in 1835.[223] Vietnam could also use an argument claiming that at least some of the southern Paracel features, like Triton Island and Herald Bank, are in closer proximity by using a line drawn equidistant between Vietnam and China, a doctrine the Philippines has used in its claim for most of the Spratly Islands.[224] Universal application of this doctrine would, however, greatly reduce Vietnam's claims in the Spratly Islands to just a few of the westerly most islands without gaining much in the Paracels. Legally, proximity and territorial contiguity arguments are given little weight in international arbitration, a precedent begun in 1925 in the Island of Palmas case.[225] Despite its historic documentation and assertions of discovery, proximity, and assumption of French claims, Vietnam's lack of physical possession of any features undermines an effective challenge to China's claim derived from physical occupation of the Paracels.

China's firm control over the Paracels may be a solution — although a military imposed one — to possession and exploitation of the Paracel Islands by adapting another Roman-based international customary law, *uti possidetis* ("as you possess, thus may you possess"). This principle allows a party to maintain as its property its current possession until its rightful owner is ascertained. In international law, this is interpreted to mean land gained (often in war) remains with the occupier unless otherwise disposed through a treaty. This principle was upheld by the ICJ in 1986 when it ruled to maintain the colonial borders inherited by independent states in the Burkina Faso vs. Mali Case.[226] This law could apply to the Paracel Islands if China keeps its present possessions, even though they were gained through conflict, unless a subsequent formal settlement is negotiated. Thus for China, not engaging with other states on this issue simply maintains the status quo for its benefit, unless enticed by other gains to reconsider its position.

United Nations Convention on the Law of the Sea and Paracels Claims.

If sovereignty over the Paracel Islands is settled through customary law, the issue of the maritime jurisdiction around them is the provision of UNCLOS. The U.S. position on this issue was revealed in 2010 by then Secretary of State Hillary Clinton at the Association of Southeast Asian Nations (ASEAN) Regional Forum (ARF):

> We believe claimants should pursue their territorial claims and accompanying rights to maritime space in accordance with the UN Convention on the *Law of the Sea.* Consistent with customary international law, legitimate claims to maritime space in the South China Sea should be derived solely from legitimate claims to land features.[227]

Unlike land claims, "sovereignty to resources in and under the sea is acquired simply by virtue of distance from coasts. This is important because it affects the role of territory as a conflict driver," as already demonstrated in this monograph.[228] Because of the importance of UNCLOS, this section discusses the key points that affect the South China Sea region, including how maritime jurisdiction is determined when originating from a land feature, the different maritime zones and their rights, and the sea and land claims that China and Vietnam have lodged using these rules.

Well-defined maritime boundaries and agreed upon rights within them are necessary to peace and stability on the ocean commons.[229] Customary maritime law, through most of history, governed space and actions on the seas by allocating three-mile-wide territorial waters from a coast, with general agreement on rights for navigation and taking of resources. Since the 1950s, however, management of the sea has become much more regulated and comprehensive through a series of international treaties culminating in UNCLOS, which was negotiated from 1973 to 1982 and took effect in 1994. This treaty gives coastal states a 12-nm territorial sea and an EEZ of limited economic control to 200-nm from the coast, and possibly a continental shelf extension to the natural limit of its seabed shelf (to a maximum of 350-nm). It also has provisions for archipelagic states to enclose the waters around and between their islands as internal waters, giving more economic and security control within their physically fragmented countries.[230] These maritime boundaries of state control are premised on the type of land feature—inhabitable land or unproductive rock—each emanates from so that issues of sovereignty, topography, and classification of a land feature determine maritime boundaries.[231]

Both Vietnam and the PRC have ratified this convention, but with reservations. Taiwan is not an eligible member, although it generally follows its rules, and the United States has signed but not ratified the trea-ty.[232] Technically UNCLOS does not apply to disputes started before it came into effect, including the Para-cels claims, but an expectation exists for signatories to abide by its provisions nonetheless.[233] Four forms of settlements are offered by UNCLOS for dispute resolution, with arbitration the assumed form since none of the states involved have yet chosen a method. States are able to opt out of some of the Law of the Sea Treaty's requirements. The PRC, for instance, does not accept compulsory procedures to settle disputes over maritime boundaries, military or legal activities in a zone, or actions of the Security Council, because those provisions might interfere with the discretion-ary sovereign powers of the state.[234] Thus, UNCLOS is a well-respected treaty that offers guidance to resolve disputes like those found in the South China Sea, but rarely does so through strict enforcement.[235]

Determination of a Habitable Island from a Rock.

After designating sovereignty over a land fea-ture—which is normally deemed beyond the pale of UNCLOS—determining the type of feature from which a maritime zone is claimed is the next step and one of the functions of the law of the sea. Inhabitable lands receive all UNCLOS maritime zones and rights, although these can be constrained by surrounding zones. Continental states receive full consideration for territorial waters and adjacent EEZ or continen-tal shelf, while islands may be assigned part or all of those areas.[236] However, what constitutes an inhabit-able island is a major concern since a qualified speck of land could accrue control over 125,000 square-nm of water column and seabed through the UNCLOS regime. Under Article 121:

> an island is a naturally formed area of land, surrounded by water, which is above water at high tide [, but] . . . Rocks which cannot sustain human habitation or economic life of their own shall have no exclusive economic zone or continental shelf.[237]

The human considerations in the island definition establishes a sub-class of islands known as "rocks" which are "barren and uninhabitable insular formations, such as cays and atolls" and receive only territorial waters and a contiguous zone around it regardless of the size of the rock.[238]

The U.S. Government compiled *Gazetteer of the Paracel Islands and Spratly Islands* has listed 18 features in the Paracels region as islands or rocks which appear to be eligible for territorial seas.[239] The respected South China Sea experts Mark Valencia, Jon Van Dyke, and Noel Ludwig note, per UNCLOS Article 121, that reefs and other features submerged at high tide garner no maritime zones "even if artificial structures are based on them," except for a 500 meter safety zone given to any artificial or temporary feature at sea.[240] Under these terms, many of the Paracel geologic features garner no maritime zones.[241] In 1975, the ICJ advised that the standard for formal displays of sovereignty, like markers and policing, is lower for uninhabited areas, which would also pertain to islands designated as rocks.[242] This monograph has deliberately not used the word "island" indiscriminately to distinguish features accurately, as used by this definition.

Because the stakes are high for how a maritime land feature is designated and the definitions used in UNCLOS are not precise, leeway is often employed to interpret this clause. Whereas physical geography may distinguish between an island and a nonisland geologic feature, human needs distinguish between a habitable island and a rock. The key question then is, "What does it take to sustain human habitation or have economic life of its own?"[243] A source of indigenous potable water might be one criterion, but would that prevent a solar powered desalinization plant from also fulfilling the requirement for human habitation? Must the island itself sustain its population with the necessities of life to be habitable, or may it be supplied from outside? Are lighthouses or navigation markers sufficient evidence of "economic life of their own"?[244] Van Dyke has argued cogently that a habitable island requires a permanent sustainable population "who are on the land area for reasons other than just to secure a claim of a distant population for the adjacent ocean resources." He explicitly discounts occupation forces and lighthouse keepers from this group.[245] He further believes, with other experts, that a population of at least 50 people could constitute a sufficiently stable community to satisfy the habitation requirement, although he has conceded that "the criterion may not inevitably require that the insular feature itself be permanently inhabited, but it would require, at a minimum, that it provide support for a regular basis by fisheries from neighboring islands. . . ."[246] The indeterminate nature of the habitable criterion leaves much room for the claimants and experts to disagree.

Under some circumstances, rocks and inhabited islands may not receive full maritime zones.[247] Rocks receive little consideration under international law to prevent them from both impinging on the similar rights of nearby islands or continents that are populous and economically active and from interfering with opportunities that should be open to all seafaring nations when located on the high seas. Additionally, this helps to reduce the incentive to "reverse engineer" a barren feature with a settlement that could claim a maritime zone that would make the feature economically viable when it was not originally.[248] Even habitable islands hold lesser status under UNCLOS when compared against the claims of a continental coast. In the 1984 ICJ case between Libya and Malta, the latter was given:

> a diminished capacity to generate maritime zones in comparison to the broad coastline of Libya . . . Thus even substantial and heavily populated islands are not the equivalent of continental landmasses in their ability to support claims over adjacent ocean space.[249]

Another point pertinent to the Paracel Islands is uninhabitable islands generate territorial waters, but do not impede the rest of the rights attributed to a larger maritime zone, like an EEZ, that may encompass it.[250] This could apply, for instance, to Triton Island, which, if it were found to at least meet the status of a rock, would generate territorial waters for the PRC, its current controller, that impinge upon Vietnam's coastal EEZ. The vague considerations that are taken into account in determining maritime boundaries and the other shortcomings of UNCLOS mean that most dispute settlements tend to be difficult, and usually considered on a case-by-case basis using precedent as a guide if submitted for review.[251]

Regarding their habitability, the Paracel Islands' conditions have proven harsh for sustaining life. In their natural state, they are tiny, low, barren islets with Rocky Island the highest in elevation at 15-m and the rest not more than 10-m, making them vulnerable to typhoons and storm surge. The islands lack fresh water beyond insufficient seasonal rainfall, and the soil consists primarily of coral, shells, and bird guano in the form of brown powder or white nodules, at one time averaging a quarter of a meter deep—little surprise, then, that the Paracels historically have sustained no indigenous human population.[252] The resulting cost of the financial and physical commitment by each of the past occupying states has been high, which explains in part why the French, Vietnamese, Japanese, and Chinese historically have been parsimonious in stationing troops in the Paracels.

The nearest case of a disputed South China Sea feature meeting the requirements for a habitable island may be Woody Island. Less than a square mile in size, it has a reputed decades-old population of about 1,000 people, consisting of military personnel, civil servants, and fishermen, most of who have temporary terms of residency.[253] To demonstrate its control over and habitability of Woody Island, the PRC has made it an administrative capital, expanded the existing runway for overseas tourists and surveillance aircraft, established a new deep water port to handle cruise liners and maritime enforcement vessels, and built a desalinization plant, 500-kilowatt solar power station, and environmentally friendly rubbish and waste water treatment facility for visitors and the increased garrison. Other improvements reported are a small 700-square-meter vegetable patch and a small coconut grove.[254]

How much Woody Island adheres to Van Dyke's concept of an island made habitable only through "reverse engineering," or his proposed criteria of an inhabitable island with a permanent population which, at a minimum, "provide support for a regular basis by fisheries from neighboring islands," is a gray area that remains one of the main points of disagreement in the region.[255] The new principles and definitions in the 1982 UNCLOS law have stirred problems of land claims to gain maritime jurisdiction in the South China Sea, which some commentators believe could best be managed by declaring the features "legally uninhabitable"[256] or pooling the maritime zones each might generate to be "shared regionally and managed by a joint development resource agency."[257] Within these bookends of open ocean and collective sovereign waters lies a continuum of maritime control by the coastal states.

Maritime Jurisdictions.

After sovereignty over a geologic feature and its type are determined, then its maritime jurisdictions are established through UNCLOS. The Law of the Sea Treaty determines how much authority a state asserts over neighboring seas as weighted by the type of land feature it is based upon and its distance from the coastline. The types of waters that may be assigned are sovereign internal waters (including closely related archipelagic and historic waters), territorial waters, contiguous zones, EEZs, sometimes a continental shelf extension, and the high seas. The high seas are the *res communis*, open for use by all states, though regulated somewhat by both customary law and UNCLOS as to how activities may be conducted. Examples of regulating the high seas include customary laws against piracy or slavery, and UNCLOS Part XI rules on the gathering of nonliving and sedentary resources from the ocean floor[258]—objections to the latter has kept the United States from ratifying the Law of the Sea Treaty. The boundaries and rights of the littoral zones are explained in this section in order to better present the potential maritime jurisdictions that are claimed in the Paracel Islands region, and their implications for U.S. interests.

Internal, Archipelagic, and Historic Sovereign Waters.

The most restrictive maritime zones are internal waters in which the state has complete sovereignty, as over its own internal lakes and land. Internal waters are adjacent national waters with access to the sea, but are inside a series of straight baselines that may connect barrier islands or cross the mouth of a narrow bay, and thus are treated as under the full sovereignty of the state.[259] Smooth coastline states might rate no internal waters, whereas countries with chains of nearby fringe islands, like the U.S. eastern seaboard or deeply indented coastline like that found in Alaska, would have internal waters from the shore to the straight baseline that connect the outermost part of these features, as stipulated in Article 7 and subsequent guidance in UNCLOS.[260] Applying this law, the United States has sovereign control over its Intracoastal Waterway on the landward side of the east coast barrier islands, but has only territorial waters control on the seaward side of those islands. Establishing a straight baseline simplifies rugged sea borders and is advantageous since it not only gains sovereign control over adjacent waters, but also, as its name implies, moves the line from which other maritime zones are measured from the shore (or normal baseline) to the straight baseline, and makes all waters landward from the straight baseline sovereign internal waters. For this reason, straight baselines often are drawn liberally, as has been done by the PRC and Vietnam, which routinely has been physically and diplomatically challenged by the United States as exceeding their rightful allowances to attain large swaths of internal water and extend their maritime zones further to sea.[261] The only exception in UNCLOS to complete sovereignty over internal waters is to allow innocent passage across recently drawn straight baselines "which had not previously been considered as such," mostly affecting states through whose waters traditional international shipping routes pass.[262] While straight baselines are applied liberally along neighboring continental shores to improve the maritime jurisdiction that may be claimed from national boundaries, their use around the Paracel Islands is also "problematic," according to Hasjim Djalal, an Indonesian diplomat who was President of the UNCLOS Assembly of the International Seabed Authority and coordinator of the informal "Track II" workshops among the South China Sea disputants.[263]

A new construct for internal waters found in UNCLOS Part IV is that of archipelagic waters, codified in part to supersede the thorny concept of historic waters.[264] Archipelagic waters specifically were intended to give fragmented island states, like Indonesia and the Philippines, authority over the waters within the confines of their archipelago as defined by its baselines.[265] Here, however, the enclosing lines are called straight archipelagic baselines, and are drawn further afield than the tips of adjacent craggy peninsulas and fringe islands. Archipelagic baselines may connect the outermost features of an archipelago with lines up to 100-nm long to enclose an area of no more than 1 to 9 land-to-water ratio.[266] Although the Paracel Islands themselves are a geographic archipelago, they would not fall under this legal regime because they are not a sovereign state, nor may the PRC use archipelagic rules with the Paracels since the mainland is not a part of the archipelago.[267] Since archipelagic rules do not apply in the Paracels, China's current declaration of its straight baselines around the Paracels may violate UNCLOS intent with 5 of 28 lines drawn longer than 24-nm in length.[268]

Historic claims, beyond those now covered under archipelagic baseline rules, are also considered internal waters under customary law. Although historic waters are not officially defined, they are occasionally referenced in UNCLOS, such as Article 10's "historic bays" or Article 15's reference to "historic title."[269] According to maritime law author L. J. Bouchez, historic waters are:

> waters over which the coastal State, contrary to the generally applicable rules of international law, clearly, effectively, continuously, and over a substantial period of time, exercises sovereign rights with the acquiescence of the community of States.[270]

Its appeal to states is that historic waters hold the sovereignty of internal waters, but do not include the innocent-transit-across-baselines caveat found in UNCLOS archipelagic waters regime. Thus, attaining historic waters status restricts freedom of navigation and curtails the exploitation of oceanic resources by the international community.[271] As preceding law, historic waters may also override UNCLOS statutes by allowing historic bays wider than 24-nm at the mouth, for instance, or giving precedence to historic waters contrary to overlapping territorial water claims which would otherwise be settled with a median line between them.[272] The motivation for a state to claim such waters is obvious, and both Vietnam and China make sweeping historic claims to large parts of the South China Sea, as previously presented.

Although some commentators assert that historic claim doctrine is obsolete or at least transitional, these claims remain very active in practice through the legal principle of *stare decisis*.[273] Nonetheless, UNCLOS was written to minimize the use of historic claims, and they are generally recognized by the international community only in exceptional circumstances.[274] As already demonstrated in the South China Sea, the Vietnamese and Chinese historic claims are not convincingly documented, lacking the continuity and long-term exercise of rights recognized by other states as defined by Bouchez. For example, it would be difficult for a state to claim historic waters where foreign ships transit on a regular basis as has routinely occurred around the Paracel Islands in the South China Sea.[275] Some officials in Beijing are reported to recognize that their sweeping claim for South China Sea historic waters conflicts with UNCLOS, and that they believe a more appropriate claim is for just the islets within its U-shaped line with their adjacent waters.[276] At least one commentator believes that Vietnamese officials are also relenting on claiming historic waters to argue its claims in terms of UNCLOS EEZ and continental shelf articles.[277] Although not taken seriously by the international community, historic waters could be a powerful and excluding disruptor if awarded to any claimant in the South China Sea.

Territorial Seas and Contiguous Zones.

Close to internal waters in concept and proximity are the maritime zones of territorial seas and contiguous waters. Territorial seas codify the customary legal practice of state control over waters within 3-nm of its shores, but UNCLOS expands this zone to up to

12-nm from the baseline. Articles 33 and 121 allow every natural feature above the high water mark to have territorial waters and up to an additional 12-nm for a contiguous zone, and China and Vietnam have established each of the UNCLOS allowed zones.[278] Territorial seas are treated as the coastal state's sovereign territory, with exclusive rights to living and nonliving resources down to and including the seabed, and enforcement of applicable national laws, but they must still allow innocent passage to transiting foreign vessels.[279] The right of innocent passage through territorial waters requires that "the peace, good order, or security of the coastal State" not be disturbed through activities like fishing, polluting, information collecting, firing weapons, or launching aircraft or boats in accordance with Article 19.[280] Coastal states may, of course, prevent noninnocent passage through its territorial waters, and may also temporarily suspend innocent passage by all foreign vessels in specific areas designated as temporary security zones in its territorial sea per Article 25.[281] The contiguous zone is a nonsovereign transitional area that allows protections for the coastal state to enforce national laws concerning customs, finance, immigration, and sanitation, but is otherwise governed as part of the less restrictive EEZ.[282] Innocent passage is not needed to transit a contiguous zone. Both zones were established to allow freedom of navigation to all vessels from any state, and to ensure good order and control over adjacent waters for the coastal state.

There are disagreements, however, over whether innocent passage applies to all vessels or excludes warships of another state, a U.S. major concern which relies on innocent passage for power projection. The 1958 convention that preceded UNCLOS clearly allowed warships innocent passage through territorial waters, and the drafting history of UNCLOS indicates the same rights.[283] UNCLOS rules for innocent passage fall under Section 3, Subsection A entitled "Rules Applicable to All Ships," which states "ships of all States, whether coastal or land-locked, enjoy the right of innocent passage through the territorial sea."[284] Despite this rule, China and Vietnam have interpreted innocent passage to exclude warships or their activities, and protest such transit vigorously.[285] Vietnam's 1980 *Enactment No. 30-CP* prohibits military ships from both its territorial sea and contiguous zone without 30 days advanced permission, although its 2012 *Law of the Sea* has relaxed the requirement to prior notification.[286] Further to sea are the PRC's permanent restricted maritime military zones, created in the 1960s, within and outside territorial waters in the Bo Hai and Yellow Sea.[287] Although these zones are north of the South China Sea, they demonstrate long-standing Chinese actions that ignore Article 25, and could also be applied around the Paracel Islands as permanent political obstructions to any foreign vessel's passage in the region.

Chinese policy since the early days of the Republic in the 1920s, after its harsh history with maritime insecurity, also bars warships' passage through its territorial seas and contiguous zones without prior consent "to safeguard its national security."[288] This was first codified in the *Declaration of the Government of the PRC on the Territorial Sea* in 1958, and reiterated in the 1992 *Law on Territorial Waters and their Contiguous Areas*, both of which explicitly included the Paracel and Spratly Islands.[289] The significance of maritime control and innocent passage for the PRC explains in part why China took more than 13 years to ratify UNCLOS and the reason for its accompanying reservations.[290] The issues of sovereignty and independence are the PRC's highest priority in its policy of *Five Principles of Peaceful Coexistence*.[291] The 1992 territorial waters law implied, and further actions have shown, that the PRC will enforce its sovereignty for its claimed Paracel and Spratly Islands.[292] Such sovereign zones, if fully enforced, would mean most or all of the sea out of limits should China or Vietnam enforce historic rights to the South China Sea islets or to historic waters.

Exclusive Economic Zones.

An innovation of modern maritime statutory law is the EEZ, by which states possessing habitable islands and continental shores economically control up to 200-nm of ocean and seabed from their baseline under Part V of UNCLOS.[293] Unlike territorial seas, however, there is no state sovereignty over this zone, just the authority to regulate the environment and natural resources, establish installations, and conduct "marine scientific research."[294] By controlling such activities, EEZs are distinguished from the less-restrictive high seas. Unlike territorial seas, navigation and over-flight of an EEZ is not subject to the coastal state's control except to enforce the authorities allowed by UNCLOS, such as resource management and pollution control.[295] Based on these provisions to manage the EEZ, the South China Sea states often challenge each other's activities in their ambiguous and overlapping claimed zones, and use their interpretations to restrict operations of foreign military craft (as already presented in this monograph).

Under customary law, the distances over which states controlled adjacent waters were short, and the amount of overlapping jurisdictions small. When UN-CLOS extended the maritime jurisdictions and created the EEZ, with states 400-nm apart becoming maritime neighbors, the problem of unilateral and overlapping EEZ claims in the Paracels resulted.[296] In such cases, delimitation establishes maritime jurisdiction boundaries between states' valid claims for territorial seas, contiguous zones, EEZs, and continental shelf.[297] To remove contention from such decisions, the earlier *1958 Geneva Conventions on the Law of the Sea* proposed a line halfway between the coastlines of overlapping jurisdictions, using the equidistance principle to delimit disputed areas that could not otherwise be settled.[298] However, in the 1970s, this straightforward method was modified in international court judgments that found even habitable lands may each carry different weight in the generation of maritime zones based on the length of their coastlines.[299] Of course, where no overlap occurs all habitable islands receive full maritime zones, but when small islands' jurisdictions abut larger islands, or larger islands' zones overlap continental landmasses, the smaller feature will receive less than full effect depending on each circumstance.[300] Weighing the amount of jurisdiction awarded in disputes to the more significant land formation is the essence of the current equitable principle, which ensures the amount of area awarded in an EEZ is proportional to the length of the coastlines involved, and not usually influenced by economic, ecological, or other characteristics.[301]

The awarding of an EEZ using these rules is important in the Paracel Islands because of the consequences for regional economic development and international navigation. Unlike territorial seas and contiguous zones, economically unviable rocks do not generate an EEZ or a continental shelf claim.[302] Under these conditions, an exposed rock would become an enclave of territorial waters for one state surrounded by the high seas or the EEZ of another state's nearby eligible landmass.[303] Since Vietnam and China claim 200-nm EEZs from their baselines, their EEZ claims conflict over controlling the region's maritime resources outside of the territorial waters given to eligible geologic features. Thus, Vietnam's EEZ would regulate the seas south of the Paracel Islands, and China's would regulate the seas around the northern features.[304] Since Vietnam included no EEZ from its claimed Paracel and Spratly Islands in its 2009 EEZ and continental shelf submissions to the UN Commission on the Limits of the Continental Shelf, its government may have determined that these land features are uninhabitable under the legal definition and merit only territorial seas.[305] This interpretation leaves an approximate 700-nm long band of high seas in the South China Sea stretching from 150-nm northwest of Woody Island to parts of Rifleman Bank in the southwestern Spratlys, which would be governed only by UNCLOS Article 87, the Freedom of the High Seas section, and the International Seabed Authority for sea floor resources.[306] China's efforts on Woody Island, however, are meant to prove that it is habitable, which, if true, would garner China more water column and seabed in the South China Sea through its Paracel occupation. Perhaps to maintain its options concerning the islands' habitability, Vietnam only made a partial submission of its UNCLOS EEZ and continental shelf claims, and may yet make further claims from its islands.[307] When interpreted under the intent of UNCLOS, establishment of EEZs is relatively straightforward in the Paracels' region.

Should PRC-occupied Woody Island be determined a habitable island, an EEZ complication arises. Woody Island's position on the edges of the Vietnamese and Chinese EEZs mean it would probably generate little EEZ to its north and southwest against continental EEZs, although that would be determined by treaty, arbitration, or international court decision. However, to the east, Woody Island could generate an EEZ in the waters of the erstwhile high seas of the northern South China Sea.[308] This additional EEZ would transfer about 40,000 square-nm from existing high seas to China's jurisdiction, including all of the shallow Macclesfield Bank from which it could derive the increased fishing and drilling potential associated with one of the world's largest sunken atolls.[309] In line with Chinese law, this enlarged EEZ would also increase China's naval buffer zone, since it prohibits foreign government vessels' transit rights in its EEZ without prior permission. In 2000, China and Vietnam negotiated a delimitation agreement, settling over a century of disputes in the Gulf of Tonkin, along with a fishing protocol, which both took effect in 2004.[310] This negotiation is a promising sign toward the resolution of overlapping claims.

If Vietnamese or Chinese historic claims are validated as internal waters, EEZs would be of diminished consequence since these sovereign seas would impinge upon the lesser authorities of an EEZ. Two vexing examples of such overlap come from China's exploration and drilling activities within Vietnam's EEZ in the southern South China Sea, starting in 1992 with the Crestone Block and continuing as recently as June 2012 with CNOOC calling for bids on blocks within 37-nm of Vietnam. China substantiates these activities through its historic claim, and they are the cause of many of the clashes between China and Vietnam.[311] China disregards Vietnamese maritime claims that conflicts with its own, exploiting resources within Vietnam's claimed EEZ while it protests when other states transit China's own EEZ claims.[312] In China's view, "a claim derived from historic rights may seem more forceful and valid in law than claims simply based upon the EEZ concept," and even if jurisdiction based on historical claims is rejected, they still offer the potential for other historic rights—like access to traditional fishing areas—that cannot be otherwise attained through UNCLOS methods.[313] The combinations of customary and statutory maritime laws with different national interpretations lead to a wide variance in the amount of control that may result, but gaining possession of the Paracels or some historical claim may garner considerable jurisdiction in the surrounding waters.

In addition to the delimitation of the EEZ, how it is enforced is also very important to the United States. In their implementing domestic laws, both the PRC and ROC claim a 200-nm EEZ and accompanying rights to regulate it under UNCLOS.[314] Should China start enforcing an EEZ around Woody Island or other occupied features in the Paracels, it would challenge foreign military vessels and aircraft to seek permission to operate within this expanded EEZ as it now does in its mainland EEZ.[315] China is essentially applying rights that apply in territorial seas to its EEZ. Through its claimed historic rights of special security interests and application of UNCLOS, the PRC requires that activities should "refrain from any threat or use of force" in the EEZ (the intent of UNCLOS definition on transit passage under Part III on straits navigation).[316] China treats its EEZ as a military buffer zone, contending that U.S. military surveillance ships and reconnaissance flights violate the spirit of UNCLOS and China's historic rights in the South China Sea and seek to restrict such activities.[317] Thus PRC laws maintain peace in its EEZ by barring foreign military vessels, citing UNCLOS Article 58 which directs that states "should comply with the laws and regulations adopted by the coastal State in accordance with the provision of this Convention."[318] If the coastal state's laws are disputed, Chinese scholars declare that deference be given to the PRC per Article 59, "taking into account the respective importance of the interests involved to the parties as well as to the international community as a whole."[319]

The United States rejects this interpretation, resulting in the PRC's restriction of the freedom of navigation through an EEZ, contending it is a minority view held by only 27 of the 161 ratifying states (significantly, Vietnam is also one of the states enforcing a restrictive EEZ).[320] Focusing on one particularly irksome activity, Chinese officials place "military survey and military information gathering . . . into the category of ocean scientific research which requires prior permission from the coastal states," thereby supplementing its objections based on regulating peace and security in adjacent waters.[321] By applying maritime law in this way, the PRC uses "international law as an adjunct to their military forces to achieve anti-access maritime objectives."[322] The triple problem of whether its occupied Paracel Islands can generate an EEZ, the amount of EEZ such features would gain against the neighboring larger landmasses, and whether foreign military vessels or certain activities are barred from an EEZ, make this a very tenuous legal argument for China.[323] However, it could be useful justification for keeping U.S. vessels out of the South China Sea from a security stand point, which China could then better defend militarily than legally. Both China and Vietnam's contentions that bar military vessels put them in a minority position within the international community, unless ever-evolving international sentiment calls again for a change to the Law of the Sea Treaty.

Continental Shelf Claims.

Although not a jurisdiction that includes a water column like the spaces discussed previously, the UNCLOS continental shelf zone is important to adjacent states for the management of nonliving resources and sedentary species on and under the seabed. Extended claims for adjacent ocean floor began with the United States in 1945, and the concept was subsequently incorporated in Article I of the 1958 *Convention on the Continental Shelf* with a limit of 200-m isobaths or the depth of exploitability.[324] By 1969, the ICJ instituted the "natural prolongation principle," which acknowledged that states had jurisdiction over a much extended continental shelf, although not necessarily from islets or minor coastal features.[325] The resulting UNCLOS articles updating this extended authority were a compromise that allowed coastal states to control the surrounding seabed to the natural length of its continental shelf or to a maximum of 350-nm from the baseline, and also gave geographically challenged states with little adjacent continental shelf at least a 200-nm EEZ that also controlled the seabed below it.[326] Under UNCLOS, states do not need to exploit or occupy the continental shelf to retain exclusive economic rights to its seabed, which includes protrusions from the seabed floor that remain submerged.[327] In Articles 78 and 79, however, it is clear that rights to the continental shelf do not affect the superjacent waters or airspace above it in order to allow navigation and the unfettered laying of submarine cables and pipelines.[328] The states around the South China Sea supported this greater control over their continental shelf that UNCLOS gave them, and have used it to their economic and political advantage.[329]

These rights over the more distant areas from the claimants' shores come with more obligations than other UNCLOS zones in how they are delimited. Here, the claiming state must first scientifically stake the extent of its continental shelf beyond 200-nm with the UN Commission on the Limits of the Continental Shelf, which then must qualify it for technical compliance.[330] This is an exacting process that must be completed within 10 years of ratification of UNCLOS. The Commission cannot qualify an extended continental shelf claim, however, if it is part of a territorial or maritime disagreement with another state.[331] Consent from the other involved states can be difficult to obtain in the contentious South China Sea environment, as seen in the 2009 joint Vietnamese-Malaysian continental shelf submission to which the PRC and the Philippines objected.[332] Further complicating delimitation of a continental shelf is the potential divergence of an EEZ water column from the continental shelf below it with each assigned to a different jurisdiction.[333] This may occur when the EEZs of a continental state and small island do not overlap, but the natural continental shelf extends out to undercut the island's EEZ, or when so negotiated. Split continental shelf and superjacent EEZ ownership are uncommon, and no resolution in the South China Sea has resorted to this yet; however, it is a possibility in the corner of Asia in which the Paracels are located.[334] These continental shelf rules make already intricate circumstances around the Paracel Islands that much more difficult to resolve.

Based on the UNCLOS definition of the extent of the continental shelf, the Paracels are located on a shelf at the 2,500-m depth level that deepens just to the northeast and southeast of the islands.[335] Using the complicated mechanism found in UNCLOS Article 76, Vietnam's declared continental shelf begins about 50-nm southeast of the center of Macclesfield Bank (but does not include the bank) and runs southwest until it joins Vietnam's claimed EEZ line approximately 250-nm due east of Phan Thiet, which approximates the equidistant line between Vietnam and the Philippines. A dotted line labeled as equidistant line on the SRV's submitted delimitation map connects its continental shelf line starting point to the southeast corner of the Paracels where it joins the intersection of the Chinese EEZ from Hainan Dao and the Vietnamese EEZ from near Quang Ngai around Bombay Reef.[336] This line does not recognize Chinese sovereignty or, at least, the habitability of the Paracels, which would mandate the use of a different line.

The PRC has made no similar declaration of its continental shelf in the South China Sea. However, such a claim might be hypothesized for China based upon its 2012 declaration in the East China Sea along the Okinawa Trough, which, when compared against a CIA map's presumed continental shelf limit and applied from Hainan Dao in the Paracels region, would indicate that the natural Chinese continental shelf does not extend as far as the Paracels themselves.[337] If the Chinese continental shelf physically falls short of the Paracels, its EEZ nonetheless has legal jurisdiction out to 200-nm from Hainan Dao, which describes an arc ending east of the Paracels. This means all of the islets are encompassed by a Chinese or Vietnamese EEZ.[338] Extending the aforementioned equidistant line from Vietnam's northernmost claimed continental shelf point to the intersection of their EEZs around Bombay Shoal to the southernmost point of their Gulf of Tonkin maritime boundary line—as agreed to by treaty in 2000—fairly splits this marine domain between China and Vietnam by using the equidistance principle.[339] This equitable division, however, puts the southern Crescent Islands in Vietnam's EEZ, thus opening the possibility that Chinese controlled islets rating 12-nm territorial seas, such as Triton or Money Islands, would carve holes into Vietnam's EEZ. Put another way, Vietnam's EEZ would intrude between China's Paracel Islands if the claimed straight archipelagic baselines encompassing them are deemed invalid.[340] Fortunately, between the deal for White Dragon Tail Island in 1957 and the delimitation of their shared Gulf of Tonkin border in 2000, communist Vietnam is the only state to have negotiated successfully maritime territory or boundary disputes with the PRC, offering the potential to do so again through an equitable division of their EEZ around the Paracels.[341]

This maritime jurisdiction overlap would be further complicated if Woody Island is found to be habitable. A legally habitable Woody Island would exert little change on the Vietnamese and Chinese equitable EEZ and continental shelf already described, based on the precedent of the Libya vs. Malta Case by the ICJ in 1985.[342] As previously explained, however, a habitable Woody Island could claim EEZ jurisdiction in the high seas of the northern South China Sea, significantly extending the reach of its occupying state to include Macclesfield Bank about 150-nm to the southeast. Since China and some of the Southeast Asian states—though not Vietnam—make territorial claims to submerged features in the South China Sea, rather than exerting maritime jurisdictional control over them as stipulated in UNCLOS, controlling a habitable Woody Island would also lay territorial claim to Macclesfield Bank under application of the Chinese interpretation of UNCLOS.[343] Although hypothetical, should China win recognition of its possession of the Paracels, receive a habitability determination for Woody Island, and continue its doctrine of claiming underwater features, China's claimed EEZ would extend across half of the South China Sea, by which it could restrict passage of foreign naval vessels into a bottleneck through its interpretation of restrictions in its EEZ.

However, as with the other forms of claims, these Chinese maritime claims have serious weaknesses. The first weakness is legal since, despite these Chinese interpretations, much of the international community does not recognize sovereignty claims to territory made through UNCLOS, a purpose for which it was not intended.[344] A more vexing problem is the ill-defined Chinese historic claim which could trump other customary and UNCLOS claims in the region. China's historic claim within its South China Sea U-shaped line includes all surface and sub-surface features.[345] This encompassing claim squarely conflicts with EEZ and continental shelf claims made by each of the ASEAN South China Sea rim states.[346] For instance, as early as 1992, the PRC created the Crestone oil exploration block around Vanguard and Prince of Wales Banks (in the southwestern South China Sea within 200-nm of the Vietnamese baseline) in order to drill within what is otherwise Vietnamese jurisdiction.[347] Such liberties persisted into 2012 when CNOOC offered nine blocks for oil and gas exploration within 37-nm of Vietnam (though it did not receive many international bids).[348] Elsewhere in the South China Sea, China's historic claim extends as far south as within 100-nm of Malaysia to include North and South Luconia Shoals, Friendship Shoals, and James Shoals; Scarborough Shoal in the Philippine EEZ, 130-nm from Subic Bay; and the entire Spratly Islands Group, which China disputes with Vietnam, Malaysia, Brunei, and the Philippines.[349] To defend its broad claims, China has disputed each continental shelf submission made to the UNCLOS Commission concerning the South China Sea,[350] and as one Chinese scholar reminds other powers: "[They] should understand that the Convention [UNCLOS] is just one of the international laws of the sea, not the only one, and thus should stop questioning the legitimacy of China's 9-dashed [U-shaped] line."[351]

If negotiated in good faith, the maritime jurisdictions of the EEZ and continental shelf around the Paracel Islands could be resolved based on coastal baseline claims, even if sovereignty over the islands themselves remains a more difficult issue. The impingement of historical claims against UNCLOS-derived claims magnifies this problem from around the Paracels to throughout the South China Sea. The amount of high seas seabed available in the South China Sea is of interest to the United States since these areas are exploitable for their resource wealth by any state, and maximizing the availability of deep sea regions and economic return from them is one of the major factors hindering the United States from ratifying UNCLOS. Should the overlapping EEZ and continental shelf claims become national jurisdictions, they would remove all the high seas in the South China Sea.[352] Thus the extended continental shelf disputes and their resolution will remain a point for the United States to monitor and influence to maintain its own interests and set precedents to its liking.

Territorial and Jurisdiction Claim Summary.

As a "semi-enclosed sea" dominated by overlapping maritime claims, the South China Sea bordering countries are enjoined by UNCLOS Article 123 to "cooperate with each other in the exercise of their rights and performance of their duties" beyond that normally expected of other maritime states.[353] The shared nature of migratory fish resources, indistinct location of energy sites and advent of lateral drilling, cumulative effect of environmental damage, competing territorial claims and rights, and tight confines that result in confused and conflicting maritime jurisdictions, demonstrate why cooperation is an ideal, if unrealized, goal in the South China Sea.[354] Although a few diplomatic advances to address these myriad regional concerns have been made along the sea's periphery, the states have more often adhered to customary and statuary legal principles that best favor their respective geopolitical positions.[355] Under this system, the coveted maritime zones of territorial seas, contiguous zones, EEZs, and extended continental shelves depend upon the determination of sovereignty over, and classification of, claimed land features, which is the core of the South China Sea islands disputes.[356] The by-product of demonstrating effective sovereign control and administration over these claims, unfortunately, has sometimes resulted in aggressive and violent enforcement of national laws and perceived international rights, which makes this an important issue to address in order to prevent miscommunication, accident, or impatience to justify the use of force to settle the disputes.

Until now, however, the disputants have mainly resorted to making outsized claims to maximize any future negotiated outcome, or strengthen their cases before going to arbitration or a tribunal.[357] China and Vietnam have asserted sovereignty through discovery and occupation, the most internationally accepted legal method,[358] and in this the PRC reigns as the current sole occupier of the Paracel archipelago. Vietnam and China also make ill-defined historic claims as another approach to territory, waters, or rights; this method is not well regarded by the international community and, in its collective judgment, lacks sufficient documentation in its application.[359] Under UNCLOS principles, the straight baselines declared by both countries along their mainland coasts probably exceed their authority, and the resulting excessive internal waters and maritime zones are protested by the United States and other countries. China's attempt at using archipelagic rules to establish a baseline around the Paracels also exceeds the intent of UNCLOS. None of the economically unproductive Paracels may themselves generate extended maritime zones; if some could, they probably would be given diminished domain against larger land masses under the equitable principle, thereby greatly reducing their significance and the importance of sovereignty over them.[360] Although China and Vietnam have ratified UNCLOS, each also takes exception to its settlement mechanisms and other select provisions that reduce the overall effectiveness of the treaty to reconcile maritime disputes.[361] Thus, although they often frame their claims and defense of those claims in terms of legal principles, neither China nor Vietnam has been willing to adjudicate their differences through existing arbitration or court structures, instead they are looking for a negotiated or political solution over which they have more control in determining results.[362]

U.S. INTERESTS AND RESPONSES TO THE ISSUES AROUND THE SOUTH CHINA SEA REGION

With this background established, it is clear that events in the South China Sea affect important U.S. interests. The information given thus far was presented to better inform policymakers about the involved states' diplomatic, military, police, and legal issues and actions. The issues are complex and contradictory, meaning any U.S. involvement needs to be well-informed and nuanced. This section reviews the most relevant U.S. interests in the South China Sea region in terms of freedom of navigation, economic activities, and the competing U.S. roles of honest brokering for peace and stability among the disputants and regional balancing of power for its security partners. Without maritime jurisdiction or territorial claims of its own in the South China Sea — but strong interests in how these issues are resolved — U.S. involvement by necessity is mostly indirect support and grounded in international law, but it is also motivated by a political component. Based on these interests, this monograph makes a few recommendations on how the United States may positively influence the situation in the South China Sea to enhance its interests and those of the disputants. Due to the underlying nature of this situation, these recommendations emphasize the diplomatic, informational, and economic elements of U.S. power over military ones.

Although President Barack Obama's administration again made the Asia-Pacific region a top U.S. priority in 2012, this region has been a major U.S. economic and security focus since Commodore Matthew

Perry opened Japan in 1854.[363] In particular, five important U.S. global interests are represented there today: protecting free and unimpeded commerce in the global commons, securing peace and stability among the states, supporting diplomacy and rules-based conduct, ensuring the U.S. military's freedom to operate in compliance with international law, and supporting U.S. allies and defense partners.[364] Then Secretary of State Hillary Clinton reiterated these interests specifically for the South China Sea region at the ARF in July 2010, emphasizing that:

> The United States, like every nation, has a national interest in freedom of navigation, open access to Asia's maritime commons, and respect for international law in the South China Sea. . . . The United States supports a collaborative diplomatic process by all claimants for resolving the various territorial disputes without coercion. We oppose the use or threat of force by any claimant. While the United States does not take sides on the competing territorial disputes over land features in the South China Sea, we believe claimants should pursue their territorial claims and accompanying rights to maritime space in accordance with the UN Convention on the Law of the Sea. Consistent with customary international law, legitimate claims to maritime space in the South China Sea should be derived solely from legitimate claims to land features.[365]

To achieve these goals, Secretary Clinton emphasized the need to cooperate in areas of common interest in trade, peace, security, and transnational problems like climate change and nuclear proliferation, especially with China.[366] However as an interested party, the United States is also maintaining a relatively balanced playing field because recent clashes in the South China Sea jeopardize "vital national interests of the

United States," as Senator John McCain and then Senator John Kerry observed to Dai Bingguo, China's Vice Minister of Foreign Affairs,[367] and U.S. involvement might make it a "little bit easier for the governments in the region to acquire the necessary political will" to resolve their disputes.[368] Increased U.S. involvement may have spurred negotiations in July 2011 when the PRC agreed with Vietnam to implement long-delayed guidelines to govern their disagreements, if for no other reason than to limit U.S. involvement.[369] In short, the United States seeks to ensure the legal rights that it and the international community should enjoy in the region, support the legitimate interests of its regional partners, and act upon common ground with China and other involved states to their mutual benefit to improve stability and prosperity in the region.[370]

U.S. Freedom of Navigation Interests.

The issue of immediate concern for the United States, because it may be the most volatile and the first national interest listed by Secretary Clinton, is freedom of navigation.[371] Since UNCLOS was under negotiation in 1979, the U.S. global Freedom of Navigation Program seeks to dispute excessive sea and airspace claims perceived to violate international law by challenging them diplomatically and physically.[372] China and Vietnam hold restrictive passage views concerning their coastal home waters—potentially China will also hold these views in its claimed territorial waters, contiguous zones, and EEZs around the Paracel Islands. These positions place it at odds with most other states' open-use positions, and, as a precedent threatens, EEZ navigation rights around the world.[373] On the other hand, China sees this as an excuse for the

United States to intervene in South China Sea issues, and protests, for instance, U.S. exercises with Vietnam and other powers in the South China Sea.[374] The PRC has more aggressively and consistently enforced EEZ restrictions than any other state, threatening freedom of navigation for all maritime states and risking armed clashes and instability, especially when backed by its advanced anti-access and area-denial capabilities.[375] After the 1995 PRC occupation of Mischief Reef in the midst of the Philippine EEZ, the United States made clear its stance for freedom of navigation throughout the South China Sea, and in 1998 specifically sent a carrier battle group near the Spratly Islands to assert American prerogatives.[376] As recently as 2012, after the Scarborough Shoal stand-off, Philippine Foreign Secretary Albert del Rosario wondered about China's aggressive stance and the future of "freedom of navigation and unimpeded commerce in the [South China Sea]."[377] Thus the United States considers these rights important for itself and for other interested parties[378]

Despite these chronic tensions, with the growth of prosperity in the region, the need for stability and security, and the pursuit of other common interests, the perspective of each party may start to converge in settling their differences. The United States has made progress toward this with Vietnam through a code of conduct concerning activities on the South China Sea, negotiations on navigation, and improved military ties.[379] This better understanding may have contributed to Vietnam relaxing its coastal EEZ transit requirements in 2012 to be more in accordance with UNCLOS standards.[380] Like Vietnam, as the PRC's economy grows and its international commitments expand, China's interests may converge with the U.S. global views in balancing broad international maritime rights with the coastal state rights that China now favors.[381] The PRC is the world's largest exporter and second largest importer of goods, and thus highly depends on the maritime commons to keep its economy growing, and it has prospered from the open shipping order assured by U.S. naval power. However, as China's dependence on seaborne trade continues, it may want to protect its own shipping and sea lines of communication rather than rely on its partner and competitor, the United States, to do so.[382] With among the largest merchant marine fleets and navies in the world, China's perspective should transition to accept the majority interpretation of UNCLOS—this means more open use of sea jurisdictions and a conventional interpretation of coastal states' rights in its EEZ and territorial sea. In 2012, PLAN vessels conducted surveillance in the U.S. EEZs around Guam and Hawaii, the latter during a naval exercise, thus experimenting with a more open interpretation of conducting military activities in a foreign EEZ.[383] Indeed U.S. interests also seem to be evolving toward embracing stronger coastal states' rights in its own EEZ for economic and environmental protection, thus converging interests may make resolving this issue easier over time and helping to enable some of the suggestions below.[384]

To spur this convergence of interests, specific steps should be taken by the United States to defuse the freedom of navigation issue, especially when the most active differences lie with China. The United States could back away from its insistence on exercising its rights to navigate in the South China Sea and its coastal waters in order to ease chronic tensions on this issue. This action was recently recommended by former U.S. National Security Advisor Zbigniew Brzezinski and debated among scholars, but doing this for long could needlessly weaken the U.S. and other states' worldwide commitment to UNCLOS open-sea provisions.[385] Instead, as the PRC takes a more involved role in ensuring stability and security in the international commons, the United States should work with China to establish a common understanding on maritime rights in coastal waters and abroad since that is ultimately in both of their interests. The United States and China already have the 1998 Military Maritime Consultative Agreement to prevent incidents between them, and—though quite imperfectly applied—it is a useful confidence-building measure.[386] In April 2014, the United States, the PRC, and 19 other Western Pacific naval powers approved a new code of conduct for naval encounters in disputed areas, the Code for Unplanned Encounters at Sea (CUES). However, the code is not legally binding and PLAN officials themselves question whether China will fully observe it.[387] To better tie the PRC to safe conduct protocols, then, the next step should follow the lead of the 1972 U.S.-Soviet Union Incidents at Sea Agreement (INCSEA).[388] This is a successful tool that avoided negative encounters between the two powers, yet complied with international law covering activities like innocent passage through coastal jurisdictions. Through uniform procedures both sides may follow and observe the other's ships, but could not interfere with their lawful passage, regardless of prior notification, cargo, arms, or type of propulsion.[389] An INCSEA agreement would overlap similar multilateral agreements, but those do not address the specific differences in interpretation between the two countries, nor contain all of the tools available in INCSEA. The mere act of negotiating such a confidence building-measure (and recognizing China as a rising power in the process) could also help soothe this sometimes difficult relationship and emphasize that such issues are not unique to the United States and China.[390] INCSEA is a practical, tested method which could be tailored to reduce tensions, support both sides' long-term interests, and accelerate a process of confidence-building between the two within the contentious South China Sea without foregoing the precepts of UNCLOS.[391]

Other forms of cooperation, both military and civilian, could also help build better understanding and trust and work toward common interests like stability, counter crime, and freedom of navigation in the region as envisioned by Secretary Clinton.[392] A telling example follows the major 2009 incident involving the USS *Impeccable*, after which such incidents decreased in part because both sides realized that cooperation on issues like North Korea and the global economic recession were more important interests they shared.[393] While many disputes over issues like Taiwan and military surveillance in the EEZ persist, both sides can build much needed trust and cooperation through existing military and civilian programs like the MMCA, and broaden to new ones to work through their differences. Existing programs to build upon include the Sino-U.S. Maritime Security Consultation mechanism, the Annual Defense Affairs Consultation mechanism, and the *Container Security Initiative* signed in 2003 to combat terrorism.[394] Recent combined sea exercises held an anti-piracy drill off the coast of Somalia in 2012 and a search and rescue exercise around Hawaii in 2013, each meant to "build trust, encourage cooperation, enhance transparency, and avoid miscalculation."[395] Because of their nature, some new initiatives would be easier to implement, such as information exchanges on piracy and terrorism, and maritime disaster mitigation plans. With increased understanding and trust, combined personnel training for humanitarian missions or counterterrorism could follow, with standardized procedures for data and awareness-sharing developed between them.[396] These could directly improve relations and indirectly support freedom of navigation and are actions that the U.S. administration and Congress could support with both China and the Southeast Asian states.[397]

The most promising military cooperation with China has been through the U.S. Coast Guard (USCG), which may be a more politically acceptable partner for other governments when emphasizing its enforcement and rescue over its military roles.[398] The various Chinese maritime enforcement agencies and the USCG have already enjoyed cooperative success through the multilateral North Pacific Coast Guard Forum; student training exchanges; detailing Chinese officers aboard USCG cutters in the North Pacific for enforcement actions against Chinese fishermen; and combined bilateral and multilateral exercises in port security, search and rescue, and law enforcement. In 2006, the USCG established permanent liaisons with maritime agencies in four Chinese ministries, solidifying a good working relationship with each.[399] Continuing this relationship, in 2013, a group of retired American admirals and maritime experts met with Chinese officials during the formative stage of the Chinese Maritime Surveillance Force to discuss its operations as a professional coast guard.[400] The U.S. Coast Guard offers other venues of cooperation and confidence-building, such as sharing its global expertise in protecting port and energy loading operations with Chinese authorities, whose country relies heavily on the safe and secure conduct of maritime energy shipments.[401] Coast

Guard cooperation with China is a model to expand to increase understanding and reduce tensions about issues both sides deem imperative.

The Department of Defense (DoD) should also play a role in establishing trust and cooperation between the United States, China, and Vietnam. A DoD-wide program to encourage military-to-military engagement through regionally aligned forces under U.S. Pacific Command (PACOM) integration would implement security assistance to enhance the military capabilities of the region's states. This should allow Vietnam and the other ASEAN countries in the South China Sea disputes to negotiate in a more level environment, build regional understanding with guidance from the Department of State, and strengthen bilateral relations for the United States to act as an honest broker. Regionally aligned forces entail specific units receiving training about a particular area before deploying there, and they may be assigned in military-to-military partnerships resulting in a better understanding by U.S. forces of local cultures, languages, geography, forces, and challenges.[402] U.S. units and individuals gain insight and establish enduring personal relations through training-focused visits in platoon to brigade size units.[403] This approach in Southeast Asia makes sense, especially since China is the most likely U.S. peer rival so that repeated engagement with the PRC and its neighbors should build trust, reduce tensions, address differences in fields like maritime access, and establish the United States as a regional conciliator.

An emphasis on using land forces for such engagement is needed because the new Air-Sea Battle doctrine concept parcels high-end missions like countering anti-access/area denial to the Air Force and Navy in the U.S. role of balancing China's power by supporting and protecting the interests of allies and partners in the region. Expanding theater engagement using regionally aligned forces also makes sense since armies tend to dominate the region's defense forces in terms of budgets, leadership, and influence. It is left to the land forces and coast guard, playing a smaller part in the defense of the South China Sea region, to support the conciliator role by building trust, capability, and relationships through the Army, Marine Corps, and special operations forces as proposed by former Under Secretary of Defense for Policy Michele Flournoy.[404] Land forces up to brigade size can be tailored to support ASEAN states through security cooperation activities without threatening China directly because of the fragmented physical geography and the defensive nature of U.S. land forces in the region.[405]

A more robust regime of exercising, education exchanges, and contingency planning for events of importance to both the United States and the PRC could slowly influence the PLA to better understand American positions and influence the United States to better understand Chinese positions, thus overcoming historic and geopolitical distrust. As one of the major arbiters over the freedom of navigation dispute within the Chinese system, better relations with the PLA would be helpful in resolving this and other issues both sides face. For U.S. Army forces, upon which the brunt of regional specialization would fall, this alignment concept follows the vision imperative in the Army Chief of Staff's 2012 *Army Strategic Planning Guidance*: "Provide modernized and ready, tailored land force capabilities to meet Combatant Commanders' requirements across the range of military operations."[406] To improve engagement with the PLA and the other armies of the region, PACOM was raised to a four star component command in 2013.[407] The benefits of regionally aligned forces include more effective interactions and support, improved U.S. understanding and interoperability during multinational actions, and better understanding by both sides to allow the United States more access and influence with partners and competitors alike.[408]

Elements of this regionally aligned force proposal exist in the U.S. Army with Special Operations and National Guard units already aligned to the Pacific region, and with the Army soon adding active duty conventional forces as well. Special Forces units have long specialized to build their competence in the world's regions as advisors and operators to improve partner states' capabilities and build interoperability and trusted relationships. The 1st Special Forces (SF) Group at Fort Bragg, North Carolina, currently operates under Special Operations Command Pacific, covering Southeast Asia, China, and the rest of the Pacific region along with the U.S. Army National Guard 19th SF Group headquartered in Draper, Utah.[409] U.S. Army civil affairs (CA) units also specialize to provide civil-military expertise to conventional forces during theater engagement and full spectrum military operations. The active duty 84th CA Battalion (CAB) at Joint Base Lewis-McCord (JBLM), Washington State, and 97th CAB at Fort Bragg also align with PACOM, as does the Army Reserve 364th CA Brigade in Portland, Oregon.[410] In 2014, as part of its greater regional alignment initiative, the U.S. Army plans to assign a soon-to-be designated conventional unit from I Corps, headquartered at JBLM, to support PACOM security cooperation and partnership building activities.[411]

Reserve component forces, when regionally specialized, offer advantages to include greater personnel stability, unique civilian expertise, and some military skills not residing in the active forces, and have thus been particularly effective at achieving high levels of trust, understanding, and cooperation with partners.[412] In PACOM, there are three long-term State Partnership Programs with Southeast Asian states, including the Hawaii and Guam Army National Guard partnered with the Armed Forces of the Philippines since 2000; the Hawaii National Guard also partnered with the Indonesian National Armed Forces in 2006;[413] and the Vietnamese military (Vietnam People's Army or PAV) and Oregon National Guard partnered in 2012.[414] The nature of the new PAV and Oregon National Guard partnership is manifest in the composition of the first Vietnamese planning delegation to Oregon in April 2013, led by an army lieutenant general and included experts in law, marine shipping, economics, medicine, port and maritime security, search and rescue, and humanitarian aid.[415] These partnerships facilitate stability and national interests by building partner capacity through exchanging military skills and experience, professional development, exercising, and interagency cooperation.[416]

This partnership is the latest step in a slowly evolving relationship between Vietnam and the United States. Following the Indochina Wars, U.S.-SRV diplomatic recognition began in 1995 with a decade of tepid and technical military interaction. However, as understanding between the two former enemies overcame their suspicions, their interactions grew. The first U.S. Navy port call visit to Vietnam occurred in 2003, followed in 2005 with increased training through the International Military Education and Training program and sharing of intelligence on terrorism and transnational crime.[417] These military capacity-building activities contributed to Vietnam seeking closer defense ties with the United States to hedge China's growing power, as demonstrated with the deployment of a U.S. aircraft carrier to Vietnam for combined naval exercises in 2011.[418] Both sides also agreed to cooperate through periodic high-level meetings, maritime security, search and rescue, discussion about peacekeeping, and humanitarian assistance and disaster relief, which the establishment of the State Partnership Program should advance.[419]

As U.S. global strategy emphasizes the Asia-Pacific region, more closely aligning land forces supporting PACOM's security and engagement plans is a needed initiative for peacetime-shaping operations in order to resort less to direct intervention.[420] However, in an era of fiscal austerity, these needed efforts must be adequately sustained and kept efficient to make them viable, be allowed time to take root and grow, and be protected against short-term budget cuts and competing strategic options.[421] One easy-to-correct flaw in the active duty conventional unit regional alignment scheme is that units are assigned to support a region for 1 year, unlike the longer-term assignments of SF, CA, and National Guard units.[422] Such an arrangement will not build adequate regional expertise, personal relations, or continuity in training and operations to achieve combatant command requirements. Even though active duty unit personnel change more often than reserve component personnel, the institutional links nonetheless remain important, and active duty units should be assigned long-term regional commitments at the brigade or battalion levels. Another consideration for the Army is that, as deployments to Central Command decrease, more units should be regionally aligned to PACOM to allow them to focus on a sub-region like the states bordering the South China Sea.[423] The current scheme has SF, CA, and conventional forces supporting PACOM from Mongolia to New Zealand, which dilutes the merits of regional specialization. Units assigned to smaller regions or even to critical countries like Vietnam, as done in the State Partnership Program, allow deeper understanding of the region, richer and more frequent contacts with a targeted group of key people, and improved continuity in programs. These alignment efforts would improve U.S. contributions to stability and security in the South China Sea region.

Other U.S. military services also engage in military-to-military activities in the region, although not regionally aligning units as well as some parts of the Army. The U.S. Navy held its fourth annual Naval Engagement Activity with Vietnam in April 2013 as part of a destroyer and rescue and salvage ship port call to Da Nang, which focused on noncombat events like search and rescue, medicine, diving and salvage operations, and seamanship skills.[424] The Marine Corps Security Training Group (MCSCG) builds partner-nation military capacity by advising U.S. units and participating countries on security training and organization, especially with units sharing a similar maritime or expeditionary mission.[425] Although MCSCG-trained units have completed some training in PACOM, more emphasis on key states like Vietnam—similar to that given in Africa and Latin America—is needed through regionally aligned forces that would better support both sides in their mutual training and engagement goals.[426] Theater engagement activities are an important part of PACOM's theater security cooperation plan using all of the military services in pursuit of U.S. national interests.

Regional alignment and specialization of units to engaging and shaping tasks does come with problems and challenges. First is to get the affected countries to accept more U.S. involvement, and hence influence, of this type. Although its past ties and an insurgent threat made the Philippines an early and enthusiastic supporter of recent U.S. engagement activities, Vietnam has been a late and careful participant because of its need to balance U.S. overtures with its complicated relationship with China and its adversarial history with the United States. For these reasons, U.S.-Vietnamese military cooperation should continue incrementally along established plans and channels that build upon past activities. Expanding search-and-rescue exercises and allowing more than one annual U.S. Navy ship visit are examples of building upon existing success.[427] The recent establishment of a partnership with the Oregon National Guard shows that Vietnam will expand into new activities if treated as an equal partner. One scholar recommends that new ideas with the Vietnamese are best broached through an exchange of information and ideas leading to mutually desired activities in areas such as humanitarian assistance, peacekeeping operations, and disaster relief—and expanding to involve more active duty U.S. Army and Marine forces.[428] Experts from the Center for Strategic and International Studies received reports from Vietnamese counterparts that Vietnam may also be interested in quietly training with U.S. Special Forces and hosting a U.S. Navy research facility.[429]

Regional specialization of U.S. units and personnel is costly and comes at the expense of some combat readiness, since engagement and combat training have limited overlap. The investment in trained personnel and established relationships would also have to be protected, requiring changes in the Army personnel system to retain experienced military members and minimize out-of-unit assignments—in essence creating a regimental system in the regionally aligned active forces.[430] Task, equipment, and personnel specialization come with a price to large unit combat skills, flexibility, and traditional force structure.[431] In a major operation elsewhere that requires the use of PACOM-aligned units, all of this specialization may be for naught, making necessary maneuver, fire, and effects skills not as strong as their more often used engagement skills.[432] In austere fiscal times, however, some risk must be assumed in strategy and force structure decisions, and U.S. Army Chief of Staff General Raymond Odierno has made it clear: "We always have to be prepared to fight our nation's wars if necessary, but in my mind, it's becoming more and more important that we utilize the Army to be effective in Phase 0, 1 and 2. . . ."[433] To mitigate these risks, the DoD planning considerations of flexibility and reversibility must be inherent qualities in the formation of any regionally aligned specialized units.[434] Some military service control over its units might also be surrendered to allow DoD to assign roles and regions to better coordinate coverage and activities among all of the branches to be more efficient and effective in their engagement.[435] In these times, one potential advantage to regionally aligned forces rotating into a region is that less infrastructure and cost is required in comparison to as many units permanently stationed overseas.[436] Ironic and indirect as it seems, military-to-military engagement, especially using regionally aligned land forces, may build the trust and influence necessary to ensure that UNCLOS-compliant freedom of navigation is allowed by the coastal states of the South China Sea.

Another very important step for the U.S. Government, to better ensure the freedom of navigation rights it now exercises, is to formally ratify the UNCLOS treaty. This step is not just to return to equal footing with other members on moral, diplomatic, and legal grounds in order to better support the rules-based-order that the United States government espouses, but also to be able to directly guide and protect U.S. interests in international fora and on the seas.[437] The United States signed UNCLOS in 1994 after successfully negotiating an amendment to the document to correct earlier concerns by the industrialized states, but has not formally ratified it through the Senate. The most important UNCLOS provisions, like maritime jurisdictions and right-of-passage, are in accord with U.S. policy so that U.S. domestic law generally adheres to UNCLOS statutes, as it also does with customary international law.[438] The Department of State and DoD both support ratification to give the United States "greater credibility in invoking the convention's rules and a greater ability to enforce them."[439] This treaty has come before the Senate several times, as recently as 2012, only to be tabled despite bipartisan support, mainly due to economic concerns with Part XI stipulations that cover the deep seabed.[440] A direct American voice in the Law of the Sea Treaty debates could advocate for freedom of navigation and other U.S. interests as international law inevitably evolves, in order to counter the historic trend to circumscribe rights on the high seas by reducing its openness and limiting areas of operations. Foreign military navigation rights through an EEZ are a prime example of such restrictions with 26 countries supporting China's and Vietnam's restrictive positions, including major maritime states like India and Brazil.[441] The Senate needs to ratify this treaty to allow the United States to defend actively its existing maritime legal interests and rights.

Another way to support freedom of navigation rights in the South China Sea is to have China and Vietnam clarify their historic claims. In the modern era of statutory maritime law, sweeping historic claims seem archaic, too incongruous to effectively adjudicate an area as openly used as the South China Sea, and the ensuing disputes unnecessarily hobble economic development and peace.[442] The International Court of Justice has conceded that customary law does not provide for a clear method of adjudicating historic claims, so each case is settled differently based on its specific merits.[443] This gives both Vietnam and China some basis for their historic claims even while the 1951 International Law Commission criteria make these claims appear weak.[444] Nonetheless, their restrictive interpretations of transit rules in conjunction with expansive Chinese and Vietnamese claims to historic waters, if enforced, could selectively close the very busy South China Sea to military and commercial traffic, which is why the United States and other maritime powers have worked to diminish the doctrine of historic waters and curtail its widespread application.[445] This is in part what Secretary Clinton meant in her earlier quote that "legitimate claims to maritime space in the South China Sea should be derived solely from legitimate claims to land features."[446]

To defuse this problem, China and Vietnam should declare what their historic rights entail — for example: waters, islands, rights to activities, or some combination — and where they are claimed, since neither country has been explicit in what it wants.[447] So far, it has cost the historic claimants little to hold these bargaining positions with such sweeping ambiguous claims, and it has become a convenient distraction and delaying tactic to a solution. The United States, along with the ASEAN parties and other maritime states, should press China and Vietnam "to particularize or justify its claim" to set the stage for serious negotiations and eventual compromise on specific historic issues.[448] Dropping notorious historic rights claims altogether, in favor of current maritime statutory law, would simplify the dispute to just occupation doctrine and UNCLOS provisions, although this is an unlikely course given the current situation in the South China Sea. Either method could successfully remove the dead weight of historic claims to allow much needed economic development around the South China Sea, while also reducing the specter of security threats that could derail other initiatives and engulf the region in violence.

Vietnam will find it difficult to best China's historic case in a legal dispute, and it cannot militarily match China's ability to back its claim with might (as proven by the physical loss of the Paracels to Chinese occupation).[449] Under the principle of *uti possidettis*, China's current occupation gives it control over the islands unless it chooses to give some up to Vietnam. On the other hand, Vietnam has a much stronger occupation presence in the disputed Spratly Islands, which China also claims in their entirety, and the Philippines, Malaysia, and Brunei claim in part. Vietnam might be convinced to transform its undefined historic claims for the steadier position under occupation and UNCLOS laws in the Spratlys, especially if given strong international support for current Vietnamese island sovereignty and coastal EEZ and continental shelf claims that comply with UNCLOS. In return,

Vietnam would concede that its historic sovereignty in the Paracels is no better than the Chinese, its ability to reverse China's occupation of the Paracels is slight (barring some unlikely catastrophic event in China), and it would gain little in maritime jurisdiction even if it did gain control over the Paracels.

Such a policy recognizing the actual situation in the South China Sea and legitimizing those positions should garner consistent U.S. support in accordance with Secretary Clinton's call for settling legitimate territorial and maritime claims using UNCLOS and accepted international customary law. Indeed, UN-CLOS provisions for the EEZ and continental shelf were meant in part to replace historic claims, and Vietnam might be a good candidate to do this.[450] To improve the deal, the international community should also support specific historic economic rights for Vietnam for well-documented activities like fishing, which would include assured access to the area but not jurisdiction over it.[451] In return for internationally recognized claims and rights, Vietnam would agree to fully abide by majority interpretations of UNCLOS to include freedom of navigation in its EEZ, innocent passage in its territorial seas, and to drop its claim to historic waters or title in the South China Sea. Indeed, Vietnam's "internationalizing" strategy in these disputes, assembling support under recognized law in favor of its positions at regional fora such as the 2010 ARF, is meant to counter Chinese claims with the weight of international consensus.[452] Although a practical, logical compromise to a complicated situation, the emotional nationalist and economic aspects of this problem will make replacing historic claims difficult under any combination of incentives that try to make more legally accepted procedures work.[453]

Unfortunately, there may be less incentive for China to clarify any of its claims in the South China Sea. There are legal and political advantages for China to obscure its historic, other customary, and UNCLOS-based claims together by "rigidly refus[ing] to clarify the basis for its claims,"[454] which are challenged in the international community.[455] Its occupation claims in the Spratlys are on literally and figuratively shifting ground, and its occupation of the Paracels was finalized by military conquest. Therefore, an ambiguous historic stance in the region allows China to shift its claim-support as circumstances dictate and not be held accountable in the context of modern international law, "even as the growth of its military and maritime assets gain physical leverage over its weaker neighbors."[456] China may use ambiguity as a way to deflect U.S. and other outside maritime states' involvement by obscuring topics to negotiate, and thereby keeping what it considers regional bilateral issues from being internationalized.[457] The lack of specificity may also result from political divides on these issues within the government of the PRC, which may make any change in policy arduous.[458] China may be playing a weak historic-claims-hand by keeping it close to its chest.

However, there may be influential elements in the Chinese government that see its international role growing and that its current restrictive navigation policy not only sets the PRC at odds with most other states, but also with its own future needs as an emerging world power requiring access to littoral regions around the world. Among its divergent agencies, the argument might prevail that the PRC should rely on its growing navy for defense of its home waters rather than weaker legalistic methods which may later be used against them, especially if mutually acceptable methods to open EEZs to navigation are made in arrangements similar to INCSEA. At least one commentator has noted that the PRC's recent legislation and policy statements seem to be part of a trend of historic waters being "gradually turned into the EEZ and continental shelf of the Paracel and Spratly archipelagos" without actually foregoing its assertions for historic rights.[459] Most parties would not want the United States to be directly involved in negotiating any such schemes, but it could, nonetheless, support such solutions indirectly through its good offices, expertise, and material support.

U.S. Economic Interests.

Open economic access to the South China Sea maritime commons is the second U.S. interest listed for the region by Secretary Clinton.[460] PACOM's regional strategy acknowledges the importance of open access to the shared commons in the Asia-Pacific region adding "that continued economic prosperity is tied to the peaceful rise of China as an economic and military power,"[461] making this economic issue one also linked to security. Within the bounds of UNCLOS, economic access includes the universal rights for commercial shipping and to exploit the natural resources of the high seas.[462] Short of open conflict or blockade, however, the only threat to commercial passage in the South China Sea is its designation as historic waters, which would subject passage to restrictions similar to transiting internal waters, worse than what foreign military craft have faced in PRC and Vietnamese EEZs. To date this remains just a possibility since neither China nor Vietnam try to regulate commercial traffic through their claimed historic waters or maritime jurisdictions.[463] The issue of commercial passage through the South China Sea is directly linked to the determination of historic waters in the region, meaning the discussion previously presented to reduce the effects of historic rights will apply, supporting U.S. economic interests as well.

If commercial navigation is not currently a problem, commercial exploitation of South China Sea resources may be. According to the UNCLOS preamble, the high seas are interpreted as:

> the area of the seabed and ocean floor and the subsoil thereof, beyond the limits of national jurisdiction, as well as its resources, [and] are the common heritage of mankind, the exploration and exploitation of which shall be carried out for the benefit of mankind.[464]

Although UNCLOS does regulate fishing and mineral extraction (the most common forms of economic use in these deep sea areas),[465] developed countries with high-end technology, expertise, and capital have an advantage in exploiting "the common heritage of mankind." For this reason, UNCLOS includes a regime through the International Seabed Authority (ISA) to regulate the remote gathering of strategic metals from the seabed floor, considered potentially the most lucrative activity of the high seas, and distribute part of the gained profits to all nations.[466] As a semi-enclosed sea, however, Article 123 also gives the bordering states rights and duties to manage, conserve, and exploit the living resources of the sea and protect the marine environment,[467] which raises questions about who will manage which parts of these high seas. None of the South China Sea parties, especially China, are likely to accept opening their sea's bounty to shared profits under ISA rules.[468] Each of the South China Sea states has demonstrated its desire to improve its claims and maximize natural resource gains from the sea, which this monograph has shown is a major factor in the disputes and violence among them.[469] U.S. interests in the economic uses of the high seas would be governed by UNCLOS if the United States joins, but potentially also by the South China Sea neighbors based on their maritime claims or cooperative administration as a semi-enclosed sea.[470]

Disregarding the historic waters issue—which would make exploitation of this sea by other states moot—the tangled claims in the South China Sea leave in doubt how much may be high sea and how much are within national jurisdictions. If measured as just EEZs from coastal baselines without any islands generating more than territorial waters—which is the position taken by Vietnam, Malaysia, and the Philippines—then high seas would be the elongated center of the South China Sea from north of Macclesfield Bank, down to and including the western Spratly Islands to southwest of Rifleman Bank.[471] Should China succeed in its claim for the Paracel Islands and prove they are habitable, the islands' position within continental EEZs mean they may generate a relatively modest zone consisting of a sector around Macclesfield Bank, which would become Chinese EEZ and reduce the size of the northern high seas area.[472] Commercial rights to sea life, mineral, and energy resources on the high seas depend in part on how territorial claims and maritime jurisdictions are delimited based on island sovereignty, because the remainder becomes high seas for any state's access. Thus the principle of maintaining openness is important as a precedent to ensure access to the high seas here and elsewhere in the world, and to maintain the peace.

U.S. economic interests face two problems then in the South China Sea: the UNCLOS rules concerning exploitation of the high seas, and how much of the high seas are available in the area. The United States has not formally ratified UNCLOS for several reasons, but objections to Part XI covering exploitation of the deep seabed is a main one because its provisions are considered statist and not free-market oriented, and the ISA is expensive and inefficient.[473] Opponents also see little gain in the South China Sea for U.S. ratification since the overlapping disputes would not only remain but have no compulsory settlement agreement, and maritime jurisdiction issues like freedom of navigation are exempt from mandatory arbitration mechanisms. Thus these political issues do not change whether the United States is a member or not.[474] The irony of opposing U.S. entry to UNCLOS is that in the nearly 30 years since it was written, no country or corporation, including the United States, has been successful in commercially mining for high seas mineral resources, but the United States, which has the world's largest aggregate EEZ, benefits from the economic and environmental protection of its littoral that UNCLOS provides.[475] By its present stance, the United States gains freedom from the ISA to potentially mine seabed resources some day since it does not need to be a member of UNCLOS to exploit international waters under customary law, but it loses the advantages of being inside the Law of the Sea Treaty system to guide it and employ its provisions for future U.S. benefit.

Of greater importance for U.S. interests than the laws covering the economic exploitation of the high seas are the regimes that may govern these waters. In addition to the different possibilities for maritime jurisdictions based on awarded sovereignty presented in this monograph, a governing regime relying on joint development of the sovereign and/or international zones of the South China Sea is possible. Although the waters around the Paracel Islands will be divided in one fashion or another between Vietnamese and Chinese EEZs, the EEZ that a habitable Woody Island might generate to just beyond Macclesfield Bank could be managed as a Joint Development Zone (JDZ) to share resources, or a less robust Joint Management Zone (JMZ) to facilitate research and measures to protect the environment and fishing stocks.[476] In these arrangements, jurisdiction claims are retained by states in disputed areas, but each state has a part in the exploration, development, or protection based on a sharing agreement in ways that could also become confidence-building measures.[477] On a small scale, a successful joint development area already operates between Vietnam and Malaysia and could serve as a model for Vietnam and China.[478] This solution fulfills Secretary Clinton's goal of land and maritime claims based on recognized international law in a collaborative diplomatic process.[479] By sharing resources and finally generating some of its economic potential, joint management is a promising solution to develop the region for both sides' benefit.

The economic concern for the United States in these schemes is whether such development in the high seas is a venture under UNCLOS or customary law provisions that recognize all states' rights, or whether the high seas are to be controlled and administered by a regional entity. If a jointly shared regional commons is formed around the Paracels through combining coastal EEZs with the convenient interpretation that maritime jurisdictions are generated from the islands, the resulting commons then pools the region's resources for mutual benefit of the claimants. This type of approach is not explicitly sanctioned in UNCLOS, but has international legal precedent in which Honduras, Nicaragua, and El Salvador were given "condominium" ownership in the Gulf of Fonseca Case. A similar combination of national maritime jurisdictions and shared claims through a condominium would eliminate the international waters southeast of the Paracels, and a much larger area if applied to the Spratly Islands.[480] China has discussed such maritime joint use options with Vietnam, but will not negotiate over the sovereignty of the Paracels.[481] Although still hypothetical, such a joint solution that liberally interprets international law to benefit regional states economically and foster peace and security in the region at the expense of the economic interests of outside parties poses a dilemma for the United States. A condominium solution may impede the potential to exploit the high seas in the region, or may introduce undetermined restrictions to navigation, both contrary to U.S. interests. On the other hand, such a solution could promote peace and stability among the states through diplomatic processes and support economic development and expand energy availability in a region where it is sorely needed. Although joint development may be China's best economic option in the South China Sea, its political and economic culture has made an equitable joint management scheme difficult to implement.[482]

A joint development or management solution would follow PRC communist party leader Deng Xiaoping's proclamation in the early-1990s that in the South China Sea "sovereignty is ours, set aside disputes, pursue joint development," a policy which subsequent Chinese leaders have embraced (during the Indonesian Track II talks, for example), but of which other leaders are wary.[483] Any joint development or governing deal in the South China Sea is burdened by the paucity of compromise and trust among the rim states as discussed in this monograph.[484] An analysis of the South China Sea situation by the respected International Crisis Group warns that:

> Joint development, while an opportunity for claimants to cooperate and thereby reduce tensions, has stalled as claimants resist China's demands that they first accept its sovereignty over disputed areas. The failure to reduce the risks of conflict, combined with the internal economic and political factors that are pushing claimants toward more assertive behavior, shows that trends in the South China Sea are moving in the wrong direction. . . . Claimants would benefit from taking concrete steps toward the joint management of hydrocarbon and fishing resources, as well as toward reaching a common ground on the development of a mechanism to mitigate or de-escalate incidents, even if they cannot agree on an overall approach to dispute resolution.[485]

As the sole occupier of the Paracels, China holds a strong position and is likely to expect attractive advantages in a joint scheme, and would only join a joint organization that is looser than the condominium solution described previously.[486] Vietnamese diplomats have had more success than others in negotiating with China on joint issues like the maritime delimitation and fishing agreements in the Gulf of Tonkin, which entered into force in 2004.[487] The two states subsequently agreed in 2006 to explore bilaterally for oil in the Gulf of Tonkin, and in 2013 expanded the exploration area and length of the agreement to 2016.[488] Since 2005, their navies have conducted a dozen joint enforcement patrols in the Gulf of Tonkin;[489] and since 2010, they have held periodic defense-security strategic dialogues to ensure peace and stability between them.[490] Timo Kivimaki suggests a transnational Sino-Vietnamese tourism project as a starting point,[491] perhaps most equitably done on the Crescent Group using Prattle, Money, or the Triton Islands, which are held by China but in or near the Vietnamese EEZ. Hasjim Djalal has observed that in the South China Sea, bilateral development agreements such as these are easier to reach than multilateral agreements.[492] These are significant efforts at joint cooperation and development in the shared Gulf of Tonkin upon which similar efforts around the Paracels, 300-nm to the southeast, could be modeled.

Although such actions benefit both countries through joint cooperation, as championed by Chairman Deng, relations between them remain complicated and difficult. Friction over development continues as already shown in the failure of the JMSU among China, Vietnam, and the Philippines, which expired in 2008 because the smaller states believed the PRC only wished to explore in disputed areas near their shores, but not in contested areas which China was unilaterally exploiting.[493] In 2013, Vietnam rejected a Chinese maritime claim south of the Gulf of Tonkin and west of the Paracels as the basis for joint energy development because it was considered solely Vietnamese. Violent incidents also routinely continue at sea between their vessels.[494] Some analysts believe that more certain and rapid financial returns will motivate companies like CNOOC to support joint development, yet its deployment of China's first deep-water drilling rig to the Paracels in 2012 and clashes near Triton Island over Haiyang Shiyou 981 in 2014 show that CNOOC, too, is willing to operate inside the dispute to support its interests.[495] Experts argue that joint partnerships lacking strong political will may be difficult while rivalry persists; as Djalal instructed, "Development efforts needed peace, stability and cooperation."[496] Because of problems so far, South China Sea scholar Stein Tonnesson recommends postponing development until after jurisdictions are delimited and shelving sovereignty issues altogether.[497] U.S. policy, however, still supports joint development, even in disputed areas, by supporting diplomatic efforts such as the start of drafting a code of conduct to the *Declaration of the Conduct of Parties in the South China Sea* (DOC) in 2011 in order to continue a diplomatic process.[498]

United States: Honest Broker or Balancer?

Based on U.S. interests and policy presented so far, how should the United States engage in the South China Sea disputes? It can play one of two roles, and over time will probably engage in both as it pursues its interests in regional stability and prosperity, navigation, and economic development, and as changing circumstances dictate.[499] The first role is that of honest broker among the disputants helping, along with other states, to resolve these thorny issues through "respect for international law . . . collaborative diplomatic process . . . without coercion . . . [and] not take sides . . ." as proposed by Secretary Clinton.[500] Secretary of Defense, Chuck Hagel, has also stressed addressing threats through such engagement.[501] The other role is that of balancer recognizing that the sovereign states in the region do not meet on a level playing field, and that U.S. commitments and national interests obligate the United States to take some parochial positions for its own benefit or to support an enduring overall solution on behalf of a regional partner.[502] These U.S. approaches compensate for the PRC strategy in which claims for land sovereignty and maritime delimitation are conducted bilaterally to gain advantage over weaker claimants, while lesser and more encompassing issues like safety, anti-crime, and environmental protection may follow a multilateral approach.[503] Brzezinski recently summed up this dual U.S. role as the "balancer and conciliator between the major powers in the East."[504] One analyst calls this balance "defensive realist logic—increasing the security of allies without threatening China directly," or "containment-lite," which supports and restrains a partner like Vietnam while also constructively engaging or deterring a sometime competitor and collaborator like China.[505] For these reasons, harmonizing these two roles is crucial to American, Vietnamese (and other ASEAN states), and Chinese long-term interests in regional peace, cooperation, and prosperity.

When it serves to advance solutions in the South China Sea, the United States should play the role of honest broker because it shares common goals and interests for peace and stability with China and the ASEAN states.[506] Since its recent rise to regional power, China and the United States keep returning to a "constructive strategic partnership," despite intermittent intervening crises, because their long-term interests ultimately overlap, and the need to manage them together continues.[507] When China joined the Treaty of Amity and Cooperation in Southeast Asia in 2003, it signaled its intent toward equality and cooperation with the members of ASEAN as part of China's co-existence approach, which has had some success in resolving land disputes elsewhere on its borders.[508] Despite its past conflicts and current disputes with China, Vietnam also relies on diplomatic negotiations, its hedging strategy of cultivating military ties with China, and its other interactions to defuse tensions with China.[509] Even with these ties, however, China has refused discussions specifically about the Paracels, although China will discuss the status of the Spratly Islands with Vietnam.[510]

The U.S. role of honest broker in the South China Sea will encourage this engagement as equals while offering the additional benefits of allowing the United States to represent general international interests in the region and provide sought-after defense cooperation to the ASEAN states to bolster their capabilities.[511] As an honest broker, U.S. policy in National Security Presidential Directive (NSPD) 41 seeks to "enhanc[e] international relationships and promot[e] the integration of U.S. allies and international and private sector partners into an improved global maritime security framework to advance common security interests in the Maritime Domain."[512] Following this line, PACOM's 2013 strategy supports multilateral approaches with regional groups like ASEAN to develop relationships that build trust and reinforce international norms, and it also engages with China to achieve a variety of common bilateral and multilateral goals.[513] Secretary Clinton especially singled out the long-awaited full code of conduct negotiations that will supplement the 2002 DOC, in which the United States as a conciliator is "prepared to facilitate initiatives and confidence building measures" among the parties.[514] Such measures build the necessary trust in the United States to help respond to crises or when support is needed, and is simply good diplomatic practice in a tense region with important U.S. interests.[515]

U.S. and regional state interests are best served with an involved United States that can play the conciliator role when needed. This monograph has outlined why U.S. interests are served this way, but so too are the interests of the regional states. Without American involvement, stronger states may assert themselves in the disputes more, while, through miscalculation or domestic pressure, weaker states may start incidents they may not be able to contain.[516] Among the regional powers, neither China nor ASEAN, with substantial direct interests in the dispute, nor Japan, with indirect interests similar to the United States but with a negative legacy that makes it distrusted in the region, can substitute in this role.[517] Indonesia, through the Track II talks it has hosted since 1990, has ably played the role of diplomatic conciliator in the South China Sea disputes, but Indonesia, too, may have maritime conflicts with China's historic claims and lacks the substantial resources that the United States can bring to influencing solutions.[518] The United States may be a good mediator because it has enough interests in the disputes to remain engaged, diplomatic power to help maintain the rule of law, important overlapping interests with each party (especially China) to be cautious and balanced, sufficient distance from the region to have no sovereignty claims and prefer local initiatives and solutions, and is willing to include all affected states in the process through programs like its Global Maritime Partnership.[519]

This U.S. stance has been called "active neutrality," although, when necessary, that includes direct actions like confronting the PRC when U.S. navigation interests are threatened, while also restraining a partner perhaps when domestic nationalist sentiment spurs a government to be too aggressive, as almost happened in 2011 and 2014 when huge demonstrations in Vietnam and prominent citizens chastised their government for being "too timid" in its responses to incidents with China.[520] The United States is thus an important factor in promoting the peaceful and prosperous environment to which China and the other Asian states have contributed and mutually benefited from, but the United States has done so by allowing the states involved to take the initiative for mediation.[521]

As shown, however, the U.S. position has not been strictly neutral, and the United States has become involved in the dispute when deemed necessary. Until the 1995 Mischief Reef incident in the Spratly Islands, the United States did not intervene in the South China Sea because the disputes did not affect global stability or major U.S. interests. Since the end of the Cold War, as the United States has perceived increasing threats to the sea lanes and potential for military conflict in the South China Sea, Chinese observers believe that U.S. policy has evolved from active neutrality to "active concern," and as a result the United States has become more willing to intervene.[522] PRC officials see a less impartial United States siding with the Southeast Asian states at its expense, at least indirectly if not in public, and that the United States may be slowly abandoning neutrality.[523] The strategic shift of focus to the Pacific Rim and East Asia is a major example of a more active and potentially parochial role for the United States.

Some ASEAN states are anxious about the uncertainty around China's growing power and possible dominance of the region.[524] Others, like Vietnam, have already found China's claims and behavior in the region to be overbearing and threatening, and quietly welcome the U.S. commitment to deter potential aggression from the PRC to ensure security and allow negotiations toward a settlement.[525] In support, South

China Sea powers have offered the United States access or basing rights, including Vietnam, allowing use of the old U.S. naval base at Cam Ranh Bay for noncombat naval ship maintenance and visits of combat ships at other ports, while regional allies have welcomed the U.S. renewed emphasis on the Asia-Pacific region.[526] Their fear is that when vital Chinese interests have been threatened, the PRC has resorted to conflict to protect them,[527] and there is a possibility that the South China Sea may prove to be one of those core Chinese interests.[528] Through its military, economic, and political power; cultivated ties with the disputants; and its own national interests, the United States alone may be the "external balancer providing security guarantees to whatever state may be attacked by another, and thereby making regional balances-of-power much less significant."[529] However, the United States must remain committed to involvement in the region and can ill afford to be inconsistent by cancelling important engagement opportunities, like three planned presidential visits since 2010 that were abandoned due to domestic U.S. incidents, which undercut the regional states' perception of the United States as a steadfast partner,[530] or President Obama's 2014 guarded foreign policy speech at West Point that left South China Sea states questioning a strong American commitment to their region.

Partiality in the disputes is due in part because the Southeast Asian states seek a counterbalance to nearby China, and the United States best serves in that role today. For example, after its reunification in 1975, Vietnam relied on the Soviet Union (until its dissolution in 1991) as an ally to counter China.[531] By 1992, ASEAN supported a U.S. military presence in the region to balance Chinese growth, and Vietnam and the other states have since improved military co-operation with the United States to reinforce that commitment.[532] To preserve its own interests and maintain the balance of power in the Asia-Pacific region, the United States needs to remain involved to protect the maritime commons of East Asia and its partners from intimidation.[533] Doing so has its challenges, however, since countering small incremental actions like an unauthorized Chinese oil rig in the Vietnamese EEZ or a bout of Chinese 'reactive assertiveness' patrolling more aggressively for fishing violations in its own claimed areas may not be a *causus belli* for the United States, but such actions accumulate to change the status quo in the South China Sea in China's favor.[534] The Obama administration has worked to promote more unity within ASEAN, which has no real defense arrangement, to better withstand Chinese pressure.[535] To this end, PACOM's strategy seeks to strengthen relationships with ASEAN and its states, and specifically "enhance our partnerships with Indonesia, Malaysia, Singapore, Vietnam, and others to advance common interests and address shared threats,"[536] while Vietnam and the Philippines have both sought stronger backing from the United States and ASEAN in their island disputes with China.[537] Brzezinski concludes that in Asia the United States should play the dual role of conciliator and regional balancer, as the United Kingdom did in nineteenth century European politics, by "mediating conflicts and offsetting power imbalances among potential rivals."[538]

American balancing actions have weighed against China when needed but usually in a way to not endanger its role as conciliator, since doing both are not mutually exclusive activities and are part of a normal process of great power cooperation and competition.[539] In 2010, the United States maneuvered the ARF agenda to make the South China Sea disputes a primary topic for multilateral, not bilateral, discussions; and at the subsequent ARF meeting in Hanoi, Secretary Clinton denounced unilateral actions in the South China Sea and supported the need for all parties to negotiate a code of conduct. This indirectly condemned China for both its aggressive actions and its recalcitrance to an already agreed-upon procedure, while offering the branch of conciliation at the same time to rectify the situation.[540] Balancing also means strengthening ASEAN military capabilities through establishing or strengthening military cooperation agreements, and forward deploying U.S. forces into East Asia with Vietnamese engagement—perhaps the fastest developing relationship in the region.[541]

The United States should continue its strategy of robust deployments of naval, air, and ground forces, and alliances and cooperation with like-minded states.[542] These moves support U.S. interests in the South China Sea as declared by Secretary Clinton, thereby "internationalizing" the disputes to the consternation of the PRC, which loses diplomatic and military advantage.[543] U.S. intervention has been overt as well, for instance, by loudly condemning Chinese actions to establish the Sansha municipality over the South China Sea islands, while not criticizing similar earlier actions by Vietnam and the Philippines.[544] In addition, the U.S. Senate in 2011 unanimously approved a nonbinding resolution voicing "grave concern" over aggressive Chinese actions.[545] U.S. officials have also described Chinese jurisdiction claims within the U-shaped line as excessive, and thereby some analysts believe "the United States is now a disputant in the South China Sea disputes."[546] However, for the

United States, such measures provide the region the military security needed for diplomacy to operate on a relatively level field, or as a past Vietnamese ambassador bluntly stated, "If the United States does not show some signs of support for the smaller countries on this issue, Vietnam will have no choice but to accommodate China. . . ."[547]

The United States must manage adroitly its dual roles. Because of its own interests and obligations, the United States should continue to play the balancer role, but needs to account for the significant benefits and risks to the region in terms of peace and stability.[548] U.S. involvement acts to deter the use of force, balancing weaker regional states' power with that of the PRC, and thereby constraining the parties to work within a diplomatic and legal framework (while also drawing the smaller states closer to the United States).[549] For instance, after Secretary Clinton's greater interest in the South China Sea at the 2010 ARF, a Vietnamese diplomat exclaimed that China did not take Vietnam seriously before, but "they talk to us now."[550] The United States must be alert, however, to not let such support embolden some states and increase regional instability.[551] U.S. support to a common ASEAN position in the South China Sea, a position pushed by Vietnam to link its Paracel Islands with the broader Spratly Islands dispute that also involves the Philippines, Malaysia, and Brunei, could be seen as hostile by the Chinese and make the region more violent.[552] U.S. support to the members of ASEAN balances China's power and allows ASEAN to rise as a regional power on its own.[553] Chinese observers believe that its bilateral engagements with the other states were beneficial to the region until U.S. provocations internationalized the disputes through "gunboat" policy.[554] Too much or misapplied U.S. support in the region will not only alienate China, but could also sow discord among the ASEAN states, which runs counter to American intentions for ASEAN unity to balance Chinese power.[555]

Because of many mutual interests and a strong economic embrace, the United States must remain delicate and agile in its involvement in the region, but it must also remain involved because there is no viable alternative state for the roles it plays. As an honest broker to the region, it offers resources and a proclivity for mediation that, in the long run, will result in solutions yielding a more stable, prosperous, and peaceful region based on the disputants' participation. As a balancer, the United States sets the conditions needed for Vietnam to engage as a bilateral equal in the spirit of international law. Because the United States does this to further its own interests in conjunction with those of China and the ASEAN states, its commitment to these goals should be significant and enduring through building trust and reinforcing international norms. The United States alone can deter aggression by any state.[556] China and the ASEAN states should accept the United States as an honest broker to keep America's role relatively neutral, and also allow it to balance to ensure better solutions are determined in equal negotiations or under international law. At the same time, the United States should recognize that the ASEAN states, including Vietnam, are also hedging their bets with military ties to the PRC.[557] Should the United States play its dual roles correctly, it can be called upon to be both mediator and deterrent.[558] Should the United States overemphasize either role, it could embolden aggression by appearing too weak to enforce stability, or too partisan to contribute to peace. The United States and China must find a way to balance their respective "integration" and "coexistance" approaches to international affairs to maintain the peace in Asia.[559] Thus Brzezinski concludes, "If the United States and China can accommodate each other on a broad range of issues, the prospects for stability in Asia will be greatly increased."[560]

CONCLUSION

The region around the Paracel Islands and the South China Sea is fraught with physical, economic, political, and military hazards. This region is important to the economies of the surrounding states in terms of the fish they eat and sell and the potential for energy resources needed to fuel their growing economies. This bonanza of riches spurs much of the outsized claims in the region that result in diplomatic and physical clashes. This is unfortunate because the conditions these confrontations create reduce outside investment in the region, squander resources through their unregulated use, and hinder the states from co-operating for their mutual economic benefit. The high flow of maritime commerce through the South China Sea is also crucial to the economic well-being of this region and the world. Although the waters around the Paracel Islands are economically important, the islands themselves are less so. China's firm—if contested—occupation of the Paracels, however, gives it a distinct advantage in the region for security purposes, and because possession of the islands may allow control over more of the surrounding waters.

Although direct military confrontations have diminished since the 1990s, civilian enforcement agencies have been active in protecting claimed spaces, sometimes employing violence resulting in deaths. Because partner countries rely on the United States to ensure stability in the South China Sea, and to address its own interests in maintaining freedom of navigation rights and economic development of the international seabed, the United States should remain engaged with the South China Sea states on issues of mutual concern. The United States has also been embroiled in the circumstances in support of partners like Vietnam through confrontation with the PRC over rights of navigation through claimed waters. The United States must be wary of both overplaying its position or having a partner do so and alienating the PRC, or allowing the PRC to use the South China Sea as a crucible in which to test American resolve or bait a trap as part of a confrontational military rise. To better address these concerns, policymakers need to understand the underlying problems and conflicting claims that threaten security and prosperity in this region.

The use of customary and UNCLOS law in establishing claims to the Paracels and surrounding waters helps explain both the perspectives of the disputants and how they have, in part, interacted with each other and the United States on the issues of rights and claims. Their legal positions are especially important for American policymakers as they inform possible solutions and suggest how to contribute to peace and prosperity in the region. Three key legal questions must be answered to help sort the disputes: sovereignty over the islets, the nature of a claimed land feature, and the delimitation of maritime jurisdiction. Sovereignty is claimed through customary law, with China and Vietnam both using historic doctrine to claim the entire South China Sea, while both have also used the doctrine of occupation to claim the Paracels. Both states support their claims with efforts at effective administration through establishing laws governing their possessions under municipal governments, economic activities, or, in the case of China, inhabiting them. The establishment of UNCLOS precepts made otherwise unproductive land features valuable. Establishing control over them using customary law has sometimes spurred clashes.

Developed to reflect modern interpretations of international law, UNCLOS offers guidance to maritime disputes in the South China Sea but is not a comprehensive solution. Once sovereignty of a land feature is determined, UNCLOS stipulates its jurisdiction over surrounding waters based on its human characteristics. This process is meant to maintain tranquility in the ocean commons through establishing various maritime zones with graduated degrees of sovereign rights for the state. Islands designated as inhabitable or economically viable accrue more consideration than uninhabitable rocks and other features making habitability of the larger Paracel Islands an important question to be resolved, whether or not the claiming states cooperate to establish a joint maritime zone.

Once sovereignty and feature type are determined, zones of authority may be established by the occupying state depending on the distance from its established shore baseline. Internal, archipelagic, and historic waters are maritime variations of near-full sovereign control, which could be disruptive to economic and navigation activities. Vietnam or China, for instance, could control most of the South China Sea if either historic claim was affirmed. Islands above the high tide mark establish territorial waters and a contiguous zone, which would carve 24-nm zones around the Paracels, but should allow innocent passage even if restricting most other maritime activities. However, Vietnam and China do not recognize innocent passage for naval ships, which makes such zones a major concern for the United States government.

Since the length of the 200-nm EEZ allows much potential overlap among land masses and islands in the semi-enclosed South China Sea, their delimitation through equidistant or equitable principles affects jurisdiction, and, like territorial waters, Vietnam and China restrict military activities within the EEZ beyond the economic regulation normally allowed. Habitability of an island is a significant issue for EEZ delimitation since only populated or economically viable islands may claim an EEZ. The awarding of an EEZ affects freedom of navigation and the potential for U.S. economic development in otherwise international waters. Although such arguments by claimants for more restrictions in these zones are tenuous, they could be useful justification to cover military actions by states such as China, which is the most active internationally in enforcing a restrictive EEZ.

Freedom of navigation in the South China Sea is the most immediate concern for the United States in order to ensure naval vessels retain all the rights of access allowed in the region under international maritime law. Current policy in China and Vietnam restricts foreign naval activities in their zones beyond that normally attributed to UNCLOS. This is a bad precedent for U.S. maritime access around the world, but the United States has options to improve the situation in the South China Sea. First, it has already signed the MMCA with the PRC and the CUES with 19 additional states to reduce the number of maritime incidents between the two countries. Concluding an INCSEA with the PRC would clarify further the rights and responsibilities between the two, especially when operating within each other's maritime jurisdictions, while also remaining fully compliant with international law and significantly reducing the potential for future clashes. Other forms of government-to-government interaction would build confidence in present and future agreements, leverage common interests—as the USCG has done so well with its PRC counterparts—and would also reduce tensions in the region to enhance freedom of navigation. Through engagement activities of regionally aligned forces, the U.S. Army could become a significant influence in making the United States both a conciliator and balancer in the region.

U.S. ratification of UNCLOS is another important step to influence the evolution of future interpretations of freedom of navigation toward more open stipulations than some of the states around the South China Sea now espouse. Although a more difficult proposition, the United States should demand the clarification of the historic claims made in the South China Sea, in order to facilitate negotiating a settlement, accelerate economic development, and remove the potential of shutting down all foreign navigation through the region. Support to Vietnam's current islet occupations in the Spratlys, its claims to coastal EEZ and continental shelf areas in compliance with UNCLOS, and specific historic economic rights could wean Vietnam from its otherwise weak historic claims, and start sincere bargaining by linking the Paracel and Spratly disputes in a comprehensive agreement. The United States has less influence to change China's position on historic rights because the ambiguity of its positions has served China well. Here, appealing to China's future role in world politics may help to change its parochial freedom of navigation perspective into a more global one like the United States holds.

Open economic access to the South China Sea maritime commons is a second U.S. interest, but one for which the solution may diverge from freedom of navigation considerations. Access to the resources of the high seas is an important enough U.S. interest to stall the ratification of UNCLOS for nearly 20 years in order to avoid the restrictions imposed on seabed mining, although this activity has yet to become commercially viable. While the United States remains outside the treaty, however, it holds less influence over how maritime law is interpreted and evolves, and thus is at a disadvantage to shape events like whether the South China Sea becomes a wholly divided and claimed sea. Such arrangements as a joint development zone or a joint management zone could stabilize the area to provide peace and the dividends of economic development for its participants. This could detract from potential U.S. economic development activities, depending on the arrangements, but supports U.S. security and economic prosperity goals for the region as well as attains a diplomatic settlement through recognized international law.

To contribute to overall stability and prosperity in the region—and its own freedom of navigation and economic interests—the United States must delicately play the roles of conciliator and balancer as circumstances require. The United States is an honest broker through "active neutrality" because it shares goals in common with the states around the South China Sea, in accord with existing U.S. policy. Although the United States may not be truly neutral, it has less direct demands in the disputes, garnered more trust than most other states, and possesses resources to bear on these problems making it a useful interlocutor in resolving problems.

In other circumstances, the United States has intervened in problems in the South China Sea in more parochial ways to balance the diplomatic field in aid of allies and defense partners, and to directly protect its freedom of navigation interests in a policy some have dubbed "active concern." Just as the U.S. honest broker role limited the demands that its partners might make in the disputes, the balancer role should deter aggressive stances by any party lest the United States throw its weight to the other side. The balancer role is also dictated because ASEAN lacks a defense arrangement by which to counter the influence of a much stronger PRC. As a balancer, the United States has improved its military relationship with Vietnam in a remarkably short time, and challenged Chinese actions which Chinese officials have complained "internationalizes" the issues. The balancing role should be minimal so as to not overshadow the conciliator role, since both are necessary roles that only the United States can play well in order to achieve the peaceful settlements toward security and economic interests that all the states ultimately want. In short, all parties should welcome a nuanced U.S. role as both conciliator—to keep the United States relatively neutral in the disputes—and balancer—to deter aggressive actions and thus support diplomatic solutions.

This monograph presented the most important economic, security, and diplomatic interests that the United States has in the region. Its involvement as described must be nuanced to balance conflicting requirements to ensure its freedom of navigation through these waters, which also reinforces similar rights around the world, and economic development interests. The balancer role ensures that the disputants may represent themselves as full sovereign states in negotiations with each other, while the United States simultaneously maintains good economic and diplomatic relations with each of the claimant states as a conciliator. For these reasons, the United States has again made the Asia-Pacific region a major focus of its stated global interests, and converging national interests between the United States and China may indicate that some progress on the issues outlined here are possible. In the end, the conflicts in the Paracel Islands and South China Sea are not for the United States to solve, but its ability to contribute, facilitate, balance, or support is necessary toward a solution from which all may benefit.

REFERENCES

Agence France-Presse (AFP). "Vietnam Refuses to Stamp New Chinese Passport." November 27, 2012. *www.google.com/hosted-news/afp/article/ALeqM5jf38Wx8pQuvIrgmrwcibPlxqOzQg?docId=C NG.fd699e45805ce0638bbada0e1806e749.71.*

_____. "U.S. Reaffirms Defense Treaty with Philippines." *The Peninsula* (Qatar), June 1, 2013. *thepeninsulaqatar.com/latest-news/239548-us-reaffirms-defence-treaty-with-philippines.html.*

Amer, Ramses. "Claims and Conflict Situations" in Timo Kivimaki, ed. *War or Peace in the South China Sea?* Copenhagen, Denmark: Nordic Institute of Asian Studies Press, 2002, pp. 24-42.

_____. "Ongoing Efforts in Conflict Management" in Timo Kivimaki, ed. *War or Peace in the South China Sea? Copenhagen, Denmark:* Nordic Institute of Asian Studies Press, 2002, pp. 117-131.

Amer, Ramses, and Timo Kivimaki. "The Political Dimension: Sources of Conflict and Stability" in Timo Kivimaki, ed. *War or Peace in the South China Sea?* Copenhagen, Denmark: Nordic Institute of Asian Studies Press, 2002, pp. 87-116.

Armed Forces Press Service (AFPS). "Oregon National Guard, Vietnam Sign Partnership Pact." November 30, 2012. *www.defense. gov/News/NewsArticle.aspx?ID=118666.*

Associated Press (AP). "Rare Protest in Vietnam Raises a Call to Curb China." *The New York Times*, June 3, 2013, p. A7.

Avery, Nerys. "China Streamlines Maritime Law Enforcement Amid Island Disputes." *Bloomberg News*, March 10, 2013. *www.bloomberg.com/news/2013-03-10/china-bolsters-maritime-law-enforcement-amid-island-disputes.html.*

Baker, John C., and David G. Wiencek. "Conclusion" in John C. Baker and David G. Wiencek, eds. *Cooperative Monitoring in the South China Sea: Satellite Imagery, Confidence-Building Measures, and the Spratly Islands Disputes.* Westport, CT: Praeger Publishers, 2002.

_____. "Introduction" in John C. Baker and David G. Wiencek, eds. *Cooperative Monitoring in the South China Sea: Satellite Imagery, Confidence-Building Measures, and the Spratly Islands Disputes*. Westport, CT: Praeger Publishers, 2002.

Baker, Roger. "China Tests Japanese and US Patience." *Stratfor*, February 26, 2013. *www.stratfor.com/weekly/china-tests-japanese-and-us-patience?utm_source=freelist-f&utm_medium =email&utm_campaign=20130226&utmterm=gweekly&utm_content =readmore&elq=8c6ebca11e10439b995e3aa98be897d4.*

Barboza, David. "China: Vietnam Alleges Attack." *New York Times*, March 27, 2013, p. A6.

Bateman, Sam. "Maritime Confidence and Security Building Measures in the Asian Pacific Region and the Law of the Sea" in J. Crawford and D. R. Rothwell, eds. *The Law of the Sea in the Asia Pacific Region*. Boston, MA: Martinus Nijhoff Publishers, 1995, pp. 223-234.

_____. "Good Order at Sea in the South China Sea" in Shicun Wu and Keyuan Zou, eds. *Maritime Security in the South China Sea: Regional Implication and International Cooperation*. Surrey, UK: Ashgate Publishing Limited, 2009, pp. 15- 33.

Bergin, Anthony. "The High Seas Regime—Pacific Trends and Developments" in J. Crawford and D. R. Rothwell, eds. *The Law of the Sea in the Asia Pacific Region*. Boston, MA: Martinus Nijhoff Publishers, 1995, pp. 183-198.

Berteau, David J. and Michael J. Green *et al. U.S. Force Posture Strategy in the Asia Pacific Region: An Independent Assessment*. Washington DC: Center for Strategic and International Studies, 2012. *csis.org/files/publication/120814_FINAL_PACOM_ optimized.pdf.*

Blasko, Dennis J. and M. Taylor Fravel. "Much Ado about the Sansha Garrison." *The Diplomat*, August 23, 2012. *thediplomat. com/2012/08/23/much-ado-about-the-sansha-garrison/?all=true.*

Boudreau, John. "China Vietnam Expand Joint Exploration Deal Amid Tension at Sea." *Bloomsberg News*, June 20, 2013. *www.bloomberg.com/news/2013-06-20/china-vietnam-expand-joint-exploration-deal-amid-tension-at-sea.html.*

_____. "Vietnam Leader in China Seeks Export Gains Amid Sea Tension." *Bloomberg News*, June 19, 2013. *www.bloomberg.com/news/2013-06-19/vietnam-leader-visiting-china-seeks-export-gain-amid-sea-tension.html.*

_____. "Vietnam Lodges China Protest over Claims of Attack on Fisherman." *Bloomberg News*, July 18, 2013. *www.bloomberg.com/news/2013-07-18/vietnam-lodges-china-protest-over-claims-of-attack-on-fishermen.html.*

British Broadcasting Company (BBC). "China Approves Military Garrison for Disputed Islands." July 22, 2013. *www.bbc.co.uk/news/world-asia-china-18949941.*

_____. "Q&A: South China Sea Dispute." *BBC News Asia,* January 22, 2013. *www.bbc.co.uk/news/world-asia-pacific-13748349.*

Brown, Peter J. "US and China Can't Calm South China Sea." *Asia Times*, June 4, 2010. *www.atimes.com/atimes/China/LF04Ad01.html.*

Brzezinski, Zbigniew. "Balancing the East, Upgrading the West: U.S. Grand Strategy in an Age of Upheaval." *Foreign Affairs*, Vol. 91, No. 1, January-February 2012, pp. 97-104.

Central Intelligence Agency (CIA). "Maritime Claims of Northeast Asia." Map 772221AI. Washington DC: CIA, July 2006.

_____. "South China Sea." Map 737328. Washington DC: CIA, December 1995.

_____. "Spratly Islands and Paracel Islands." Map 801947. Washington DC: CIA, April 1992.

_____. *The 2012 World Factbook.* Washington DC: CIA, 2012. *www.cia.gov/library/publications/the-world-factbook/geos/ni.html.*

Chamberlain, Robert M. "Back to Reality, Why Land Power Trumps in the National Rebalance toward Asia." *Armed Forces Journal*, May 2013. *www.armedforcesjournal.com/archive/issue/2013/05/toc.*

Chan, Irene, and Mingjiang Li. "Political Will and Joint Development in the South China Sea" draft document. Recent Development of the South China Sea Dispute Conference, Haikou China. December 2012. *www.nanhai.org.cn/include_lc/upload/UploadFiles/20131291011846088.pdf.*

Chan, Minnie. "Major Development Plan for Woody Island Unveiled." *South China Morning Post*, November 4, 2012. *www.scmp.com/news/china/article/1074996/major-development-plan-woody-island-unveiled.*

Chang, Andrei. "Analysis: China's Air-Sea Buildup." *Space War*, September 26, 2008. *www.spacewar.com/reports/Analysis_Chinas_air-sea_buildup_999.html.*

Chief of Naval Operations. "United States/Russian Federation Incidents as Sea and Dangerous Military Activities Agreement" OPNAVINST 5711.96C. Washington DC: Headquarters, U.S. Navy N3/N5, November 10, 2008. *www.fas.org/irp/doddir/navy/opnavinst/5711_96c.pdf.*

Chinkin, Christine. "Dispute Resolution and the *Law of the Sea*: Regional Problems and Prospects" in J. Crawford and D. R. Rothwell, eds. *The Law of the Sea in the Asia Pacific Region*. Boston, MA: Martinus Nijhoff Publishers, 1995, pp. 237-262.

Chu, Tingoo. "The Guano Deposit of the Western Islands (Hsisatao) or Paracel Reefs." *Bulletin of the Geological Society of China* 8, No. 2, June 1929, pp. 91-95.

Chua, Baizhen. "China Offers Oil-Exploration Blocks Near Disputed Waters." *Bloomberg News*, August 28, 2012. *www.bloomberg.com/news/2012-08-28/china-offers-oil-exploration-blocks-near-disputed-waters-1-.html.*

Ciorciari, John David. *The Limits of Alignment: Southeast Asia and the Great Powers since 1975.* Washington DC: Georgetown University Press, 2010.

Civil Affairs Association. "Active Component Army Civil Affairs Units." undated. *www.civilaffairsassoc.org/civilaffairsassociation/our-nations-civil-affairs-units/active-component-army-civil-affairs-units/.*

Clapper, James R. "Statement for the Record, Worldwide Threat Assessment of the U.S. Intelligence Community." Washington DC: Senate Select Committee on Intelligence, March 12, 2013.

Clarke, Ryan. *Chinese Energy Security: The Myth of the PLAN's Frontline Status.* Carlisle, PA: Strategic Studies Institute, U.S. Army War College, August 2010. *www.strategicstudiesinstitute.army.mil/pdffiles/pub1012.pdf.*

Clinton, Hillary Rodham. "Remarks at Press Availability." Hanoi, Vietnam: National Convention Center, July 23, 2010. *www.state.gov/secretary/rm/2010/07/145095.htm.*

Cohen, Michael. "Philippines, U.S. Confirm US Navy's Return to Subic Bay." *IHS Jane's Defence Weekly*, October 10, 2012. *www.janes.com/article/13538/philippines-us-confirm-us-navy-s-return-to-subic-bay.*

Cohen, Warren I. "China's Power Paradox." *The National Interest*, Vol. 38, Spring 2006, pp. 129-133.

Colby, Elbridge. "Don't Sweat AirSea Battle." *The National Interest,* July 31, 2013. *nationalinterest.org/commentary/dont-sweat-airsea-battle-8804.*

Collins, D. "China Counters U.S. Asia-Pivot Strategy. Fortifies Island Military Base." *China Money Report*, August 13, 2012. *www.thechinamoneyreport.com/2012/08/13/china-counters-u-s-asia-pivot-strategy-fortifies-island-military-base/.*

_____. "Fish Wars 2: The Empire is About to Strike Back." *The China Money Report*, April 18, 2013. *www.thechinamoneyreport.com/2013/04/18/fish-wars-2-the-empire-is-about-to-strike-back/.*

Collins, Gabriel B. "China's Dependence on the Global Maritime Commons" in Andrew S. Erickson, Lyle J. Goldstein, and Nan Li, eds. *China, the United States, and 21st Century Sea Power.* Newport, RI: Naval Institute Press, 2010, pp. 14-37.

Columbia Encyclopedia. "Paracel Islands." *The Columbia Electronic Encyclopedia,* 2012. *www.encyclopedia.com/doc/1E1-Paracell.html.*

Cox, Dan. "An Enhanced Plan for Regionally Aligning Brigades Using Human Terrain Systems." *Small Wars Journal,* June 14, 2012. *smallwarsjournal.com/jrnl/art/an-enhanced-plan-for-regionally-aligning-brigades-using-human-terrain-systems.*

Crawford, James and Donald R. Rothwell. "Prospects for the *Law of the Sea* in the Asia Pacific Region" in J. Crawford and D. R. Rothwell, eds. *The Law of the Sea in the Asia Pacific Region,* eds. Boston, MA: Martinus Nijhoff Publishers, 1995, pp. 263-274.

Djalal, Hasjim. *Preventive Diplomacy in Southeast Asia: Lessons Learned.* Jakarta, Indonesia: The Habibie Center, 2002.

_____. "South China Sea Island Disputes" in Myron H. Nordquist and John Norton Moore, eds. *Security Flashpoints: Oil, Islands, Sea Access and Military Confrontation,* The Hague, The Netherlands: Martinus Nijhoff Publishers, 1998, pp. 109-134.

Dodds, Klaus. "Paracel Islands." *Geographical Magazine,* Vol. 82, No. 6, June 2010, pp. 14.

Dolven, Ben, Shirley A. Kan, and Mark E. Manyin. *Maritime Territorial Disputes in East Asia: Issues for Congress.* Washington DC: Congressional Research Service, January 30, 2013. *www.hsdl.org/?view&did=730456.*

Dueck, Colin. "The Return of Geopolitics." Washington DC: Foreign Policy Research Institute, July 27, 2013. *www.realclearworld.com/articles/2013/07/27/the_return_of_geopolitics_105345.html.*

Dunnigan, James. "If It Works for Special Forces . . ." *Strategy Page*, October 8, 2012. *www.strategypage.com/dls/articles/If-It-Works-For-Special-Forces...-10-8-2012.asp.*

Dutton, Peter A. "Charting the Course: Sino-American Naval Cooperation to Enhance Governance and Security" in Andrew S. Erickson, Lyle J. Goldstein, and Nan Li, eds. *China, the United States, and 21st Century Sea Power*, Newport, RI: Naval Institute Press, 2010, pp. 197-235.

Erickson, Andrew S. "Chinese Views of America's New Maritime Strategy" in Andrew S. Erickson, Lyle J. Goldstein, and Nan Li, eds. *China, the United States, and 21st Century Sea Power*, Newport, RI: Naval Institute Press, 2010, pp. 428-470.

Erikson, Andrew S. and Lyle J. Goldstein. "Introduction: In the Same Boat Together" in Andrew S. Erickson, Lyle J. Goldstein, and Nan Li, eds. *China, the United States, and 21st Century Sea Power*, Newport, RI: Naval Institute Press, 2010, pp. ix-xxix.

Forbes, Randy. "China. There, I Said It." *PacNet* 34 (Pacific Forum Center for Strategic and International Studies), June 5, 2012. *www.pacforum.org.*

Fravel, M. Taylor. "Chapter II: Maritime Security in the South China Sea and the Competition over Maritime Rights" in Patrick M. Cronin, ed. *Cooperation from Strength: The United States, China and the South China Sea*, Washington DC: Center for a New American Security, January 2012. *www.cnas.org/files/documents/publications/CNAS_CooperationFromStrength_Cronin_1.pdf.*

_____. *Strong Borders, Secure Nation: Cooperation and Conflict in China's Territorial Disputes.* Princeton, NJ: Princeton University Press, 2008.

Global Security. "364th Civil Affairs Brigade (Airborne)." Alexandria, VA: *GlobalSecurity.org*, undated. *www.globalsecurity.org/military/agency/army/364ca-bde.htm.*

_____. "Spratly Islands Conflicting Claims." Alexandria, VA: *GlobalSecurity.org*, undated. *www.globalsecurity.org/military/world/war/spratly-conflict.htm.*

Goldstein, Lyle J. "Improving Chinese Maritime Enforcement Capabilities" in Andrew S. Erickson, Lyle J. Goldstein, and Nan Li, eds. *China, the United States, and 21st Century Sea Power*, Newport, RI: Naval Institute Press, 2010, pp. 126-154.

Greenfield, Jeanette. "China and the *Law of the Sea*" in J. Crawford and D. R. Rothwell, eds. *The Law of the Sea in the Asia Pacific Region*, Boston, MA: Martinus Nijhoff Publishers, 1995, pp. 21-40.

Griffin, Steve. "Regionally-Aligned Brigades: There's More to This Plan Than Meets the Eye." *Small Wars Journal*, September 19, 2012. *smallwarsjournal.com/jrnl/art/regionally-aligned-brigades-theres-more-to-this-plan-than-meets-the-eye*.

Griffiths, David N. "Challenges in the Development of Military-to-Military Relationships" in Andrew S. Erickson, Lyle J. Goldstein, and Nan Li, eds. *China, the United States, and 21st Century Sea Power*, Newport, RI: Naval Institute Press, 2010, pp. 38-56.

Ha, K. Oanh. "Vietnam Protests China's Planned Paracel Islands Sailboat Race." *Bloomberg News*, March 30, 2012. *www.bloomberg.com/news/2012-03-31/vietnam-protests-china-s-planned-paracel-islands-sailboat-race.html*.

Ha, Van Ngac. "The January 19, 1974 Naval Battle for the Paracels against the People's Republic of China Navy in the East Sea." Ha Manh Chi, trans., January 2013. *vnnavydallas.com/tailieu/hoang_sa_01_19_1974.pdf*.

Hackett, Bob, Sander Kingsepp, and Anthony Tully. "Japanese Occupation South China Sea Islands." *Rising Storm – The Imperial Japanese Navy and China*, 2012. *www.combinedfleet.com/SouthChinaSea_t.htm*.

Higgins, Andrew. "In South China Sea, a Dispute over Energy." *Washington Post*, September 7, 2011. *www.washingtonpost.com/world/asia-pacific/in-south-china-sea-a-vnnavydallas.com/tailieu/hoang_sa_01_19_1974.pdf*.

Hong, Nong. *UNCLOS and Ocean Dispute Settlement: Law and Politics in the South China Sea*. New York: Routledge, 2011.

Hua, Judy and Chen Aizyu. "China's CNOOC Tenders another 26 Offshore Blocks, Many in South China Sea." *Reuters*, August 28, 2012. *www.reuters.com/article/2012/08/28/china-cnooc-blocks-idUSL4E8JS03R20120828*.

Hughes, Margaret. "USMC Forms MCTAG; Consolidates Reconnaissance Training." *Small Wars Journal*, November 19, 2007. *smallwarsjournal.com/blog/usmc-forms-mctag*.

Huynh, Loi. "Vietnam: New National Law Intensifies International Dispute." Washington DC: The Law Library of Congress, July 19, 2012. *www.loc.gov/lawweb/servlet/lloc_news?disp3_l205403248_text*.

International Seabed Authority. "Contractors." Kingston, Jamaica. *www.isa.org.jm/en/scientific/exploration/contractors*.

Jin, Yongming. "How to Resolve the South China Sea Issue." *China Daily*, July 7, 2011. *www.chinadaily.com.cn/cndy/2011-07/07/content_12850748.htm*.

Johnson, Constance. "China/Vietnam: South China Sea Agreement." Washington DC: The Law Library of Congress, October 11, 2011. *www.loc.gov/lawweb/servlet/lloc_news?disp3_l205402849_text*.

Joyner, Christopher C. "The Spratly Islands Dispute: Legal Issues and Prospects for Diplomatic Accommodation" in John C. Baker and David G. Wiencek, eds. *Cooperative Monitoring in the South China Sea: Satellite Imagery, Confidence-Building Measures, and the Spratly Islands Disputes*, Westport, CT: Praeger Publishers, 2002.

Kaplan, Robert D. "The Geography of Chinese Power—How Far Can Beijing Reach on Land and at Sea?" *Foreign Affairs*, Vol. 89, No. 3, May-June 2010, pp. 22-41.

_____. "The South China Sea is the Future of Conflict." *Foreign Policy*, Vol. 188, 2011, pp. 76-85.

Kate, Daniel Ten, and David Lerman. "Hagel Set for Vietnam Embrace as Wary Asia Eyes Rising China." *Bloomberg News*, May 31, 2013. *www.bloomberg.com/news/2013-05-30/hagel-set-for-vietnam-embrace-as-asian-leaders-eye-rising-china.html.*

Kiesow, Ingolf. *China's Quest for Energy: Impact upon Foreign and Security Policy.* Stockholm, Sweden: Swedish Defence Research Agency, November 2004.

Kivimaki, Timo. "Conclusion" in *War or Peace in the South China Sea?* Copenhagen, Denmark: Nordic Institute of Asian Studies Press, 2002, pp. 165-169.

_____. "Introduction" in Timo Kivimaki, ed. *War or Peace in the South China Sea?* Copenhagen, Denmark: Nordic Institute of Asian Studies Press, 2002, pp. 1-5.

Kivimaki, Timo, Liselotte Odgaard, and Stein Tonnesson. "What Could be Done?" in Timo Kivimaki, ed. *War or Peace in the South China Sea?* Copenhagen, Denmark: Nordic Institute of Asian Studies Press, 2002, pp. 131-164.

Koh, Quintella. "China-Vietnam Row Heats Up over Competing Claims." *Rigzone*, July 2, 2012. *www.rigzone.com/news/oil_gas/a/119013/ChinaVietnam_Row_Heats_Up_Over_Competing_Offshore_Claims.*

Koivurova, Timo. "Power Politics or Orderly Development?" in Sanford Silverburg, ed. *International Law,* Boulder, CO: Westview Press, 2011, pp. 362-375.

Kreisher, Otto. "DOD Too Cautious: 'We Have to be Willing to Fail,' Says Flournoy." *AOL Defense.Com,* December 12, 2012. *defense.aol.com/2012/12/12/dod-too-cautious-we-have-to-be-willing-to-fail-says-flournoy.*

Lai, David. Interview, February 21, 2013, Carlisle, PA.

_____. *The United States and China in Power Transition.* Carlisle, PA: Strategic Studies Institute, U.S. Army War College, December 2011.

Laude, Jaime. "US Troops Can Use Clark, Subic Bases." *The Philippine Star*, June 6, 2012. *www.ajdigitaledition.com/pdfs/ PDF/2012_LA/2012_06_09/2012_LA_06_09_A%2014.pdf.*

Law on the Exclusive Economic Zone and the Continental Shelf of the Republic of China. Taipei, Republic of China: Government of the Republic of China, January 21, 1998. *en.wikisource.org/wiki/ Law_on_the_Exclusive_Economic_Zone_and_the_Continental_Shelf_ of_the_Republic_of_China.*

Lee, Matthew. "US Takes Aim at China, Ups Naval Aid to SE Asia." *Associated Press,* December 16, 2013. *news.yahoo.com/us-takes-aim-china-ups-naval-aid-se-105727402--politics.html*

Lohman, Walter. *The Trap of China-ASEAN Military Cooperation.* Washington DC: The Heritage Foundation, May 2007. *www. heritage.org/research/reports/2007/05/the-trap-of-china-asean-military-cooperation.*

Ma, Rongsheng. "Geostrategic Thinking on Land-and-Sea Integration." *China Military Science Journal,* Vol. 1, No. 1, 2012, pp. 57-62.

MacKinnon, Mark. "Dangerous Nationalism on the South China Sea." *The Globe and Mail (Canada),* September 10, 2012. *m.theglobeandmail.com/news/world/worldview/dangerous-national-ism-on-the-south-china-sea/article4106336/?service=mobile.*

Mahnken, Thomas G. *Asia in the Balance: Transforming US Military Strategy in Asia.* Washington DC: American Enterprise Institute, May 2012. *www.aei.org/files/2012/05/31/-asia-in-the-balance-transforming-us-military-strategy-in-asia_134736206767.pdf.*

McAvoy, Audrey. "Chinese Ships Visit Hawaii for Exercises with U.S." *Associated Press,* September 9, 2013. *www.military.com/ daily-news/2013/09/09/chinese-ships-visit-hawaii-for-exercises-with-us.html?comp=7000023468025&rank=1.*

McLeary, Paul. "U.S. Unit's Africa Deployment Will Test New Regional Concept." *Defense News Online,* September 26, 2012. *www.defensenews.com/article/20120926/DEFREG04/309260003/U-S-Unit-8217-s-Africa-Deployment-Will-Test-New-Regional-Concept.*

McVadon, Eric A. "Humanitarian Operations: A Window to US-China Maritime Cooperation" in Andrew S. Erickson, Lyle J. Goldstein, and Nan Li, eds. *China, the United States, and 21st Century Sea Power*, Newport, RI: Naval Institute Press, 2010, pp. 252-305.

Metz, Steven. "Strategic Horizons: U.S. Must Change its Thinking on Conflict in Asia." *World Politics Review*, December 12, 2012. *www.worldpoliticsreview.com/articles/12561/strategic-horizons-u-s-must-change-its-thinking-on-conflict-in-asia*.

Moller, Bjorn. "The Military Aspects of the Disputes" in Timo Kivimaki, ed. *War or Peace in the South China Sea?* Copenhagen, Denmark: Nordic Institute of Asian Studies Press, 2002, pp. 62-86.

Moreland, Bernard. "US-China Civil Maritime Operational Engagement" in Andrew S. Erickson, Lyle J. Goldstein, and Nan Li, eds. *China, the United States, and 21st Century Sea Power*, Newport, RI: Naval Institute Press, 2010, pp. 154-171.

Ness, Tom. "Dangers to the Environment" in Timo Kivimaki, ed. *War or Peace in the South China Sea?* Copenhagen, Denmark: Nordic Institute of Asian Studies Press, 2002, pp. 43-53.

Nguyen, Hong Thao. "Sovereignty over Paracel and Spratly Archipelagoes." *Thanh Nien Daily*, April 14, 2013. *southeastasiansea.wordpress.com/2013/04/13/international-law-and-sovereignty-over-the-paracel-and-spratly-archipelagoes-part-16/*.

Odgaard, Liselotte. "Between Integration and Coexistence US-Chinese Strategies of International Order." *Strategic Studies Quarterly*, Vol. 17, No. 1, Spring 2013, pp. 16-40.

Odierno, Raymond T. *2012 Army Strategic Planning Guidance.* Washington DC: U.S. Department of the Army, April 19, 2012. *usarmy.vo.llnwd.net/e2/c/downloads/243816.pdf*.

Oil and Gas Journal Editors. "South China Sea Contested Areas Poorly Endowed, EIA says." *Oil and Gas Journal*, April 3, 2013. *www.ogj.com/articles/2013/04/south-china-sea-contested-areas-poorly-endowed--eia-says.html*.

Ong, David M. "The 1979 and 1990 Malaysia-Thailand Joint Development Agreements: A Model for International Legal Co-operation in Common Offshore Petroleum Deposits?" *The International Journal of Marine and Coastal Law*, Vol, 14, No. 2, 1999, pp. 207-217.

O'Rourke, Ronald O. *China Naval Modernization: Implications for U.S. Navy Capabilities — Background and Issues for Congress*. Washington DC: Congressional Research Service, December 10, 2012. *www.fas.org/sgp/crs/row/RL33153.pdf*.

_____. *Maritime Territorial and Exclusive Economic Zone (EEZ) Disputes Involving China: Issues for Congress*. Washington DC: Congressional Research Service, August 9, 2013. *www.fas.org/sgp/crs/row/R42784.pdf*.

Paal, Douglas H. "Dangerous Shoals: US Policy in the South China Sea." Washington, DC: Carnegie Endowment for International Peace, August 11, 2012. *carnegieendowment.org/2012/08/11/dangerous-shoals-u.s.-policy-in-south-china-sea/dc0c*.

_____. "Territorial Disputes in Asian Waters." Washington, DC: Carnegie Endowment for International Peace, October 16, 2012. *carnegieendowment.org/2012/10/16/territorial-disputes-in-asian-waters/e1ez*.

Page, Jeremy. "China Won't Necessarily Observe New Conduct Code for Navies," *The Wall Street Journal*, April 23, 2014. *online.wsj.com/news/articles/SB10001424052702304788404579519303809875852*.

Paik, Jin-Hyun. "East Asia and the *Law of the Sea*" in James Crawford and D. R. Rothwell, eds. *The Law of the Sea in the Asian Pacific Region*, Boston, MA: Martinus Nijhoff Publishers, 1995, pp. 7-20.

Pan, Chengxin. "Is the South China Sea a New 'Dangerous Ground' for US-China Rivalry?" *EastAsiaForum*, May 24, 2011. *www.eastasiaforum.org/2011/05/24/is-the-south-china-sea-a-new-dangerous-ground-for-us-china-rivalry/*.

"Paracel Islands." Encyclopedia Britannica, undated. *www. britannica.com/EBchecked/topic/442423/Paracel-Islands.*

"Paracel Islands." *List of Countries of the World,* undated, *www. listofcountriesoftheworld.com/pf.html.*

"Paracel Islands." *Nota Bene,* Youth Research Group, undated. *nbenegroup.com/territory/sisha_en.html.*

Pazzibugan, Dona and Norman Bordadora. "'It's West Philippine Sea': Gov't, AFP Use It Now to Refer to Disputed Spratly Area." *Philippine Daily Inquirer,* June 11, 2011. *newsinfo. inquirer.net/13833/%e2%80%98it%e2%80%99s-west-philippine-sea%e2%80%99.*

Peoples Republic of China. "China, U.S. Pledge to Build Constructive Strategic Partnership." Washington DC: Embassy of the People's Republic of China, April 1999. *www.china-embassy.org/eng/zmgx/zysj/zrjfm/t36212.htm.*

_____. "Declaration of the Government of the People's Republic of China on the Baselines of the Territorial Sea of the People's Republic of China." Beijing, China: Foreign Ministry, May 15, 1996. *www.un.org/depts/los/LEGISLATIONANDTREATIES/PDFFILES/DEPOSIT/chn_mzn7_1996.pdf.*

_____. *Exclusive Economic Zone and Continental Shelf Act.* Beijing, China: Standing Committee of the Ninth National People's Congress, June 26, 1998, article 12. *www.un.org/Depts/los/LEGISLATIONANDTREATIES/PDFFILES/chn_1998_eez_act.pdf.*

_____. "Executive Summary." *Submission by the People's Republic of China Concerning the Outer Limits of the Continental Shelf beyond 200 Nautical Miles in Part of the East Sea.* Beijing, China: People's Republic of China, December 14, 2012. *www.un.org/depts/los/clcs_new/submissions_files/chn63_12/executive%20summary_EN.pdf.*

Perlez, Jane. "Chinese, with Revamped Force, Make Presence Known in East China Sea." *The New York Times,* July 28, 2013, p. A9.

Perlez, Jane. "China and Vietnam Point Fingers after Clash in South China Sea." *The New York Times*, May 27, 2014. *www.nytimes.com/2014/05/28/world/asia/vietnam.html?partner=rss&emc=rss&_r=0.*

Ratman, Gopal. "Cam Ranh Bay Lures Panetta Seeking Return to Vietnam Port." *Bloomberg News*, June 4, 2012. *www.bloomberg.com/news/2012-06-04/cam-ranh-bay-lures-panetta-seeking-u-s-return-to-vietnam-port.html.*

Robinson, Amber. "USARPAC Becomes 4-Star Headquarters during Change of Command." Washington DC: U.S. Army Public Affairs Office, July 3, 2013. *www.army.mil/article/106821/.*

Robson, Seth. "China's Tactics Turning Off Asian Neighbors." *Stars and Stripes*, June 25, 2013. *www.military.com/daily-news/2013/06/25/chinas-tactics-turning-off-asian-neighbors.html?ESRC=airforce-a.nl.*

"Roiling the Waters: Tensions Rise Between China and Vietnam in the South China Sea." *The Economist*, July 7, 2012. *www.economist.com/node/21558262.*

Rudd, Kevin. "A New Road Map for U.S-Chinese Relations." *Foreign Affairs*, Vol. 92, No. 2, March-April 2013, pp. 9-15.

Rufe, Roger. "Statement of Roger Rufe, President of the Ocean Conservancy {Private}." Testimony before the Senate Committee on Foreign Relations, Washington DC, October 21, 2003. *www.foreign.senate.gov/imo/media/doc/RufeTestimony031021.pdf.*

Sanderson, Henry. "Xi Calls for Boosting China's Navy as Army Marks Anniversary." *Bloomberg News*, August 1, 2013. *www.bloomberg.com/news/2013-08-01/xi-calls-for-boosting-china-s-navy-as-military-marks-anniversary.html.*

Sen, Ashish Kuman. "Taiwan-Philippines Dispute Erupts after Fisherman's Killing." *The Washington Times*, May 20, 2012. *www.washingtontimes.com/news/2013/may/20/taiwan-philippines-dispute-erupts-after-fishermans/?page=all.*

Shearer, Ivan. "Navigation Issues in the Asian Pacific Region" in James Crawford and D. R. Rothwell, eds. *The Law of the Sea in the Asian Pacific Region*, Boston, MA: Martinus Nijhoff Publishers, 1995, pp. 199-222.

Shen, Jianming. "Territorial Aspects of the South China Sea Islands Disputes" in Myron H. Nordquist and John Norton Moore, eds. *Security Flashpoints: Oil, Islands, Sea Access and Military Confrontation*, The Hague, The Netherlands: Martinus Nijhoff Publishers, 1998, pp. 139-218.

Socialist Republic of Vietnam. "Executive Summary." *Submission to the Commission on the Limits of the Continental Shelf Pursuant to Article 76, Paragraph 8 of the United Nations Convention on the Law of the Sea.* Hanoi, Vietnam: Ministry of Foreign Affairs, April 2009. *www.un.org/depts/los/clcs_new/submissions_files/vnm37_09/vnm 2009n_executivesummary.pdf.*

The South China Sea, Vol. I, Regional Responses, Asia Report 223. Beijing, China/Jakarta, Indonesia/Brussels, Belgium: International Crisis Group, April 23, 2012. *www.crisisgroup.org/~/media/Files/asia/north-east-asia/223-stirring-up-the-south-china-sea-i.pdf.*

The South China Sea, Vol. II, Regional Responses, Asia Report 229. Beijing, China/Jakarta, Indonesia/Brussels, Belgium: International Crisis Group, July 24, 2012. *www.crisisgroup.org/en/regions/asia/north-east-asia/china/229-stirring-up-the-south-china-sea-ii-regional-responses.aspx.*

Spegele, Brian. "Rhetoric Rises on South China Sea Standoff." *The Wall Street Journal (Online)*, May 8, 2012. *contacto-latino.com/archvs/news13/4413232/rhetoric-rises-on-south-china-sea-standoff-wall-street-journal/.*

Spitzer, Kirk. "New Garrison, Old Troubles in the South China Sea." *Time Magazine*, July 26, 2013. *nation.time.com/2012/07/26/new-garrison-old-troubles-in-the-south-china-seas/.*

Stern, Lewis M. "U.S.-Vietnam Defense Relations: Deepening Ties, Adding Relevance." *Strategic Forum*. No. 246, 2009. *usacac.army.mil/cac2/call/docs/10-51/ch_6.asp.*

Studeman, Michael. "Calculating China's Advances in the South China Sea: Identifying the Triggers of Expansion." *Naval War College Review,* Vol. 51, No. 2, Spring 1998. *www.globalsecurity.org/military/library/report/1998/art5-sp8.htm.*

Sutter, Robert and Chin Hao Huang. "China-Southeast Asia Relations: Managing Rising Tension in the South China Sea." *Comparative Connections,* Vol. 13, No. 2, September 2011, pp. 67-78.

Swaine, Michael D. and M. Taylor Fravel. "China's Assertive Behavior—Part One: On 'Core Interests'," *China Leadership Monitor,* Vol. 34, Winter 2011, pp. 1-14. *www.carnegieendowment.org/files/CLM34MS_FINAL.pdf.*

_____. "China's Assertive Behavior—Part Two: The Maritime Periphery." *China Leadership Monitor,* Vol. 35, Summer 2011, pp. 1-29. *carnegieendowment.org/2011/06/24/china-s-assertive-behavior-part-two-maritime-periphery/1c6.*

Tan, Michelle. "1st Regionally Aligned BCT to Deploy to Africa." *Military Times,* February 20, 2013. *www.militarytimes.com/article/20130220/NEWS/302200333/1st-regionally-aligned-BCT-deploy-Africa.*

_____. "Army Assigns 4-Star, 79,000 Troops to US-ARPAC." *Army Times,* June 4, 2013. *www.armytimes.com/article/20130604/NEWS/306040003/Army-assigns-4-star-79-000-troops-USARPAC.*

Tonnesson, Stein. "Geopolitics and Maritime Territorial Disputes in East Asia." *Contemporary Southeast Asia,* Vol. 32, No. 1, April 2010, pp. 111-113.

_____. "The Economic Dimension: Natural Resources and Sea Lanes" in Timo Kivimaki, ed. *War or Peace in the South China Sea?* Copenhagen, Denmark: Nordic Institute of Asian Studies Press, 2002, pp. 54-60.

_____. "The History of the Dispute" in Timo Kivimaki, ed. *War or Peace in the South China Sea?* Copenhagen, Denmark: Nordic Institute of Asian Studies Press, 2002, pp. 6-23.

Townsend-Gault, Ian. "Legal and Political Perspectives on Sovereignty over the Spratly Islands" in Knut Snildal, ed. *Perspectives on the Conflict in the South China Sea* (Workshop Proceedings), ed. Oslo, Norway: Center for Development and the Environment, University of Oslo, 1999, p. 11.

Trillanes, Antonio F. IV. "The Baseline Issue: A Position Paper." Manila, The Philippines: Congress of the Philippines, undated (circa 2008). *verafiles.org/docs/trillanes-position-paper.pdf.*

United Nations. *1958 Geneva Conventions on the Law of the Sea.* Geneva, Switzerland: United Nations International Law Commission, April 29, 1958. *untreaty.un.org/cod/avl/ha/gclos/gclos.html.*

_____. "Submissions, through the Secretary-General of the United Nations, to the Commission on the Limits of the Continental Shelf, Pursuant to Article 76, Paragraph 8, of the *United Nations Convention on the Law of the Sea* of 10 December 1982." New York: UN Division for Ocean Affairs and the *Law of the Sea,* updated September 4, 2013. *www.un.org/depts/los/clcs_new/commission_submissions.htm.*

_____. *UNCLOS Declarations and Statements.* New York: UN Division for Ocean Affairs and the *Law of the Sea,* April 10, 2013. *www.un.org/depts/los/convention_agreements/convention_declarations.htm.*

_____. *United Nations Convention on the Law of the Sea.* New York: UN Division for Ocean Affairs and the *Law of the Sea,* December 10, 1982. *www.un.org/Depts/los/convention_agreements/texts/unclos/unclos_e.pdf.*

U.S. Army. "Regional Alignment in Joint and Combined Exercises." *Stand To,* August 28, 2013. *www.army.mil/standto/archive_2013-08-28/?s_cid=standto.*

U.S. Army National Guard. "Oregon National Guard Wraps Up State Partnership Program Workshop with Vietnamese Delegation." Washington DC: US Army National Guard, April 25, 2013. *www.nationalguard.mil/news/archives/2013/04/042513-Oregon.aspx.*

U.S. Defense Mapping Agency. *Gazetteer of the Paracel Islands and Spratly Islands: Names Approved by the United States Board on Geographic Names*. Washington, DC: Defense Mapping Agency, 1987.

U.S. Department of Defense. *Maritime Claims Reference Manual*, DoD 2005.1-M. Washington DC: Under Secretary of Defense for Policy, June 23, 2005. *www.jag.navy.mil/organization/documents/mcrm/vietnam.pdf*.

U.S. Department of Defense and Department of State. *Foreign Military Training and DoD Engagement Activities of Interest, 2009-10*. Washington DC: U.S. Department of Defense and Department of State, 2010. *www.state.gov/t/pm/rls/rpt/fmtrpt/*.

U.S. Department of State. *Maritime Security and Navigation*. Washington DC: Bureau of Oceans and International Environment, undated. *www.state.gov/e/oes/ocns/opa/maritimesecurity/*.

_____. "Straight Baselines Claim: China" in *Limits in the Seas*, No. 117. Washington DC: Bureau of Oceans and International Environmental and Scientific Affairs, July 9, 1996. *www.state.gov/documents/organization/57692.pdf*.

_____. "Straight Baselines Claim: Vietnam" in *Limits in the Seas* No. 99. Washington DC: Bureau of Oceans and International Environmental and Scientific Affairs, December 12, 1983. *www.state.gov/documents/organization/58573.pdf*.

U.S. Energy Information Administration. "China." Washington DC, September 4, 2012. *www.eia.gov/countries/country-data.cfm?fips=CH*.

_____. "Contested Areas of South China Sea Likely Have Few Conventional Oil and Gas Resources." Washington DC, April 3, 2013. *www.eia.gov/todayinenergy/detail.cfm?id=10651*.

_____. "Potential of Gas Hydrates is Great, But Practical Development is Far Off." Washington DC, November 7, 2012. *www.eia.gov/todayinenergy/detail.cfm?id=8690*.

_____. "South China Sea." Washington DC, February 7, 2013. *www.eia.gov/countries/regions-topics.cfm?fips=SCS*.

U.S. Government. *National Security Presidential Directive 41, Maritime Security Policy.* Washington DC: The White House, December 21, 2004. *www.fas.org/irp/offdocs/nspd/nspd41.pdf*.

U.S. Government Accountability Office. *State Partnership Program: Improved Oversight, Guidance, and Training Needed for National Guard's Efforts with Foreign Partners.* Washington DC: U.S. Government Accountability Office, May 2012. *www.gao.gov/assets/600/590840.pdf*.

U.S. Navy Task Force 73 Public Affairs. "U.S. Navy Begins Fourth Annual Naval Engagement Activity with Vietnam." Fort Smith, HI: U.S. Pacific Fleet, April 23, 2013. *www.pacom.mil/media/news/2013/04/23-usnavy-4th-annual-naval-engagement-with-vietnam.shtml*.

U.S. Pacific Command. *USPACOM Strategy.* Camp Smith, HI: U.S. Pacific Command, January 22, 2013.

USLegal. "Res Nullius Law & Legal Definition." *USLegal,* undated. *definitions.uslegal.com/r/res-nullius/*.

_____. "Terra Nullius Law & Legal Definition." *USLegal,* undated. *definitions.uslegal.com/t/terra-nullius/*.

_____. "Uti Possidetis Law & Legal Definition." *USLegal,* undated. *definitions.uslegal.com/u/uti-possidetis/*.

Valencia, Mark J. "The Spratly Islands: Dangerous Ground in the South China Sea." *Pacific Review,* Vol. 1, No. 4, 1988, pp. 438-443.

Valencia, Mark J., Jon M. Van Dyke, and Noel A. Ludwig. *Sharing the Resources of the South China Sea.* The Hague, The Netherlands: Martinus Nijhoff Publishers, 1997.

Vandiver, John. "AFRICOM First to Test New Regional Brigade Concept." *Stars and Stripes,* May 17, 2012. *www.stripes.com/news/africom-first-to-test-new-regional-brigade-concept-1.177476*.

Van Dyke, Jon M. and Dale L. Bennett. "Islands and the Delimitation of Ocean Space in the South China Seas" in Elisabeth Mann Borgese, Norton Ginsburg, and Joseph R. Morgan, eds. *Ocean Yearbook 10*, Chicago, IL: University of Chicago Press, 1993, pp. 54-89.

Vergun, David. "Army Partnering for Peace." U.S. Army New Service, October 25, 2012. *www.army.mil/article/90010/Army_partnering_for_peace_security/*.

Vidas, Davor. "The UN Convention on the *Law of the Sea*, the European Union, and the Rule of Law" in Sanford Silverburg, ed. *International Law*, Boulder, CO: Westview Press, 2011, pp. 318-361.

"Vietnam: Naval Strategy and the South China Sea." *Stratfor*, March 18, 2013. *www.stratfor.com/sample/analysis/vietnam-naval-strategy-and-south-china-sea*.

Villard, Brian. "U.S. Marine Corps Security Cooperation Group: Partnering with Foreign Militaries to Enhance Global Stability and Security." *The Official Web Site of the U.S. Marine Corps*, October 3, 2011. *www.mcscg.marines.mil/News/NewsArticleDisplay/tabid/2925/Article/70823/us-marine-corps-security-cooperation-group-partnering-with-foreign-militaries-t.aspx*.

Wang, Jisi. "China's Search for a Grand Strategy: A Rising Great Power Finds Its Way." *Foreign Affairs*, Vol. 90, No. 2, March-April 2011, pp. 68-79.

West's Encyclopedia of American Law. "Southeast Asia Treaty Organization." Farmington Hills, MI: The Gale Group, 2008. *legal-dictionary.thefreedictionary.com/Southeast+Asia+Collective+Defense+Treaty*.

Wiencek, David G. and John C. Baker. "Security Risks of a South China Sea Conflict" in John C. Baker and David G. Wiencek, eds. *Cooperative Monitoring in the South China Sea: Satellite Imagery, Confidence-Building Measures, and the Spratly Islands Disputes*, Westport, CT: Praeger Publishers, 2002.

Wikipedia. "Da Nang." *Wikipedia.org*, undated. *en.wikipedia.org/wiki/Da_Nang*.

_____. "Manganese Nodule." *Wikipedia.org*, undated. *en.wikipedia.org/wiki/Manganese_nodule*.

_____. "Money Island." *Wikipedia.org*, undated. *en.m.wikipedia.org/wiki/Money_Island,_Paracel_Islands*.

_____. "Taiping Island." *Wikipedia.org*, undated. *en.wikipedia.org/wiki/Taiping_(island)*.

_____. "Uti Possidetis." *Wikipedia.org*, undated. *en.wikipedia.org/wiki/Uti_possidetis*.

_____. "Woody Island." *Wikipedia.org*, undated. *en.wikipedia.org/wiki/Woody_Island_(South_China_Sea)*.

Wong, Edward. "Q & A: M. Taylor Fravel on China's Dispute with Vietnam." Sinosphere Blog, *The New York Times*, May 8, 2014. *sinosphere.blogs.nytimes.com/2014/05/08/q-and-a-m-taylor-fravel-on-chinas-dispute-with-vietnam/?_php=true&_type=blogs&_r=0*.

Wu, Shicun. "Opportunities and Challenges for China-US Cooperation in the South China Sea" in Andrew S. Erickson, Lyle J. Goldstein, and Nan Li, eds. *China, the United States, and 21stCentury Sea Power,* Newport, RI: Naval Institute Press, 2010, pp. 365-376.

Wu, Shicun and Keyuan Zou. "Maritime Security in the South China Sea: Cooperation and Implications" in Shicun Wu and Keyuan Zou, eds. *Maritime Security in the South China Sea: Regional Implication and International Cooperation,* Surrey, UK: Ashgate Publishing Limited, 2009, pp. 1-12.

Wu, Xinbo. *China and the United States: Core Interests, Common Interests, and Partnership.* Washington DC: United States Institute of Peace, June 2011.

_____. *US Security Policy in Asia: Implications for China-US Relations.* Washington DC: Brookings Institute, September 2000. *www.brookings.edu/research/papers/2000/09/northeastasia-xinbo*.

Wuestner, Scott G. *Building Partner Capacity/Security Force Assistance: A New Structural Paradigm.* Carlisle, PA: Strategic Studies Institute, U.S. Army War College, 2009. *www.strategicstudies institute.army.mil/pubs/display.cfm?pubID=880.*

Xue, Guifang. "China and the *Law of the Sea*: A Sino-US Maritime Cooperation Perspective" in Andrew S. Erickson, Lyle J. Goldstein, and Nan Li, eds. *China, the United States, and 21st Century Sea Power*, Newport, RI: Naval Institute Press, 2010, pp. 175-196.

Yang, Yi. "A PLA Navy Perspective on Maritime Security Cooperation" in Andrew S. Erickson, Lyle J. Goldstein, and Nan Li, eds. *China, the United States, and 21st Century Sea Power*, Newport, RI: Naval Institute Press, 2010, pp. 488-497.

Yoon, Sukjoon. "An Aircraft Carrier's Relevance to China's A2/AD Strategy." *PakNet*, November 13, 2012. *strategicstudyindia. blogspot.com/2012/11/an-aircraft-carriers-relevance-to.html.*

Yu, Wanli. "The American Factor in China's Maritime Strategy" in Andrew S. Erickson, Lyle J. Goldstein, and Nan Li, eds. *China, the United States, and 21st Century Sea Power*, Newport, RI: Naval Institute Press, 2010, pp. 471-487.

Zha, Daojiong. "China's Energy Security and Its International Relations." *The China and Eurasia Forum Quarterly*, Vol. 3, No. 3, November 2005, p. 49.

Zhu, Huayou. "Enhancing Sino-US Maritime Security Cooperation in Southeast Asia" in Andrew S. Erickson, Lyle J. Goldstein, and Nan Li, eds. *China, the United States, and 21st Century Sea Power*, Newport, RI: Naval Institute Press, 2010, pp. 377-384.

Zhuang, Jianzhong. "China's Maritime Development and US-China Cooperation" in Andrew S. Erickson, Lyle J. Goldstein, and Nan Li, eds. *China, the United States, and 21st Century Sea Power*, Newport, RI: Naval Institute Press, 2010, pp. 1-13.

ENDNOTES

1.The Paracel Islands are known as Quân Đâo Hoàng Sa in Vietnamese (Hoang Sa Islands) and Xisha Qundao (西沙群島) in Chinese (Xisha Islands). Each of the islands referenced herein also have Vietnamese and Chinese equivalents, but the standard names from the U.S. Board of Geographic Names are used throughout. U.S. Defense Mapping Agency (USDMA), *Gazetteer of the Paracel Islands and Spratly Islands: Names Approved by the United States Board on Geographic Names,* Washington, DC: Defense Mapping Agency, 1987.

2. The number of features counted in the South China Sea varies widely. In this monograph, the term "features" casts a wide net over any piece of land close to or above the water surface that affects navigation. Terms like islands, islets, shoals, reefs, banks, cays, sands, and rocks are more technical geographic terms which are defined when needed in this analysis. The approximate number of 130 features given for the Paracels is based on the number listed for the Paracel Islands in the *CIA World Factbook.* The U.S. Board on Geographic Names lists 28 named features, while Nong Hong references 15 significant Paracel islets, reefs, and shoals. Vietnam claims more than 3,000 land features in the South China Sea. USDMA; Nong Hong, UNCLOS *and Ocean Dispute Settlement: Law and Politics in the South China Sea,* New York: Routledge, 2011, p. 55; Ben Dolven, Shirley A. Kan, and Mark E. Manyin, *Maritime Territorial Disputes in East Asia: Issues for Congress,* Washington DC: Congressional Research Service, January 30, 2013, available from *www.hsdl.org/?view&did=730456; The 2012 World Factbook,* Washington DC: Central Intelligence Agency (CIA), 2012, "Paracel Islands," available from *www.cia.gov/library/publications/the-world-factbook/geos/pf.html;* "Spratly Islands and Paracel Islands" Map 801947, Washington DC: CIA, April 1992; and Socialist Republic of Vietnam (SRV), "Executive Summary," *Submission to the Commission on the Limits of the Continental Shelf Pursuant to Article 76, Paragraph 8 of the United Nations Convention on the Law of the Sea,* Hanoi, Vietnam: Ministry of Foreign Affairs, April 2009, p. 1, available from *www.un.org/depts/los/clcs_new/submissions_files/vnm37_09/vnm2009n_executivesummary.pdf.*

3. "Spratly Islands and Paracel Islands" Map; and CIA, *World Factbook,* "Paracel Islands." Woody Island is the largest in the

group and covers about .43 square-nm (about 1.6 square kilometers or 400 acres), with Duncan Island .12, Pattle Island .08, and Palm and Rocky Islands each .02 square-nm of area, for example. Tingoo Chu, "The Guano Deposit of the Western Islands (Hsisatao) or Paracel Reefs," *Bulletin of the Geological Society of China*, Vol. 8, No. 2, June 1929, pp. 91-92; and "Straight Baselines Claim: China," *Limits in the Seas*, No. 117, Washington DC: U.S. Department of State (USDOS), Bureau of Oceans and International Environmental and Scientific Affairs, July 9, 1996, available from *www. state.gov/documents/organization/57692.pdf.*

4. Jeanette Greenfield, "China and the *Law of the Sea,*" J. Crawford and D. R. Rothwell, eds., *The Law of the Sea in the Asia Pacific Region*, Boston, MA: Martinus Nijhoff Publishers, 1995, pp. 26-27; Chu, p. 92; and CIA, "Spratly Islands and Paracel Islands" Map.

5. Greenfield, pp. 34-35; and "Maritime Claims of Northeast Asia" Map 772221AI, Washington DC: CIA, July 2006.

6. Mark J. Valencia, Jon M. Van Dyke, and Noel A. Ludwig, *Sharing the Resources of the South China Sea,* The Hague, The Netherlands: Martinus Nijhoff Publishers, 1997, p. 187.

7. Tom Ness, "Dangers to the Environment," Timo Kivimaki, ed., *War or Peace in the South China Sea?* Copenhagen, Denmark: Nordic Institute of Asian Studies Press, 2002, p. 44.

8. Not all of the seafood reported here originated in the South China Sea, but this sea is a major source. *The South China Sea (II): Regional Responses* Asia Report 229, Beijing, China/Jakarta, Indonesia/Brussels, Belgium: International Crisis Group (ICG), July 24, 2012, p. 16, available from *www.crisisgroup.org/en/regions/asia/ north-east-asia/china/229-stirring-up-the-south-china-sea-ii-regional-responses.aspx;* and Dolven, Kan, and Manyin, p. 20.

9. CIA, *World Factbook*, "Paracel Islands"; Greenfield, p. 26; and D. Collins, "Fish Wars 2: The Empire is About to Strike Back," *The China Money Report*, April 18, 2013, available from *www. thechinamoneyreport.com/2013/04/18/fish-wars-2-the-empire-is-about-to-strike-back/.*

10. Hong, p. 220; and Valencia, Van Dyke, and Ludwig, p. 188.

11. Valencia, Van Dyke, and Ludwig, p. 188; *The South China Sea (II)*, ICG, p. ii; and John C. Baker and David G. Wiencek, "Introduction," John C. Baker and David G. Wiencek, eds., *Cooperative Monitoring in the South China Sea: Satellite Imagery, Confidence-Building Measures, and the Spratly Islands Disputes*, Westport, CT: Praeger Publishers, 2002.

12. M. Taylor Fravel, "Chapter II: Maritime Security in the South China Sea and the Competition over Maritime Rights," Patrick M. Cronin, ed., *Cooperation from Strength: The United States, China and the South China Sea*, Washington, DC: Center for a New American Security, January 2012, p. 37, available from *www.cnas. org/files/documents/publications/CNAS_CooperationFromStrength_ Cronin_1.pdf*; D. Collins, "Fish Wars 2"; *South China Sea (II)*, ICG, p. 13; and James R. Clapper, "Statement for the Record, Worldwide Threat Assessment of the U.S. Intelligence Community," Washington DC: Senate Select Committee on Intelligence, March 12, 2013, p. 10.

13. Robert D. Kaplan, "The Geography of Chinese Power— How Far Can Beijing Reach on Land and at Sea?" *Foreign Affairs*, Vol. 89, No. 3, May/June 2010, pp. 37-38; Hong, p. 5; and Chengxin Pan, "Is the South China Sea a New 'Dangerous Ground' for US-China Rivalry?" *EastAsiaForum*, May 24, 2011, available from *www.eastasiaforum.org/2011/05/24/is-the-south-china-sea-a-new-dangerous-ground-for-us-china-rivalry/*.

14. CIA, *World Factbook*, "Paracel Islands"; "Paracel Islands," *Nota Bene*, Youth Research Group, undated, available from *nbene-group.com/territory/sisha_en.html*; Baizhen Chua, "China Offers Oil-Exploration Blocks Near Disputed Waters," *Bloomberg News*, August 28, 2012, available from *www.bloomberg.com/news/2012-08-28/china-offers-oil-exploration-blocks-near-disputed-waters-1-.html*; Klaus Dodds, "Paracel Islands," *Geographical Magazine*, Vol. 82, No. 6, June 2010, p. 14; and Ramses Amer, "Ongoing Efforts in Conflict Management," Timo Kivimaki, ed., *War or Peace in the South China Sea?* Copenhagen, Denmark: Nordic Institute of Asian Studies Press, 2002, p. 120.

15. "South China Sea," Washington, DC: U.S. Energy Information Administration (USEIA), February 7, 2013, available from *www.eia.gov/countries/regions-topics.cfm?fips=SCS*; and *Oil and Gas*

Journal Editors, "South China Sea Contested Areas Poorly Endowed, EIA says," *Oil and Gas Journal*, April 3, 2013, available from *www.ogj.com/articles/2013/04/south-china-sea-contested-areas-poorly-endowed--eia-says.html*.

16. Methane hydrates are also known as natural gas hydrates or flammable ice. Hong, p. 75.

17. "Contested Areas of South China Sea Likely Have Few Conventional Oil and Gas Resources," Washington, DC: USEIA, April 3, 2013, available from *www.eia.gov/todayinenergy/detail.cfm?id=10651*; and "Potential of Gas Hydrates is Great, But Practical Development is Far Off," Washington, DC: USEIA, November 7, 2012, available from *www.eia.gov/todayinenergy/detail.cfm?id=8690*.

18. "South China Sea," USEIA.

19. *Ibid.*; and Dolven, Kan, and Manyin, p. 22.

20. Andrew Higgins, "In South China Sea, a Dispute over Energy," *The Washington Post*, September 7, 2011, available from *www.washingtonpost.com/world/asia-pacific/in-south-china-sea-a-dispute-over-energy/2011/09/07/gIQA0PrQaK_story.html*.

21. "South China Sea," USEIA; and Edward Wong, "Q & A: M. Taylor Fravel on China's Dispute with Vietnam," Sinosphere Blog, *The New York Times*, May 8, 2014, available from *sinosphere.blogs.nytimes.com/2014/05/08/q-and-a-m-taylor-fravel-on-chinas-dispute-with-vietnam/?_php=true&_type=blogs&_r=0*.

22. The Jiangnan Basin is found in the western part of the Gulf of Tonkin, and Wan'an is off the coast of central Vietnam. Both are located on the continental shelf of Vietnam, and both areas are claimed by Vietnam and China. Quintella Koh, "China-Vietnam Row Heats Up over Competing Claims," *Rigzone*, July 2, 2012, available from *www.rigzone.com/news/oil_gas/a/119013/ChinaVietnam_Row_Heats_Up_Over_Competing_Offshore_Claims*; Chua; and "South China Sea," USEIA.

23. The Benton Block was originally developed by the U.S. Creston Company in 1992 and is still sometimes referred to as

the Crestone Block. "South China Sea," USEIA; Michael Studeman, "Calculating China's Advances in the South China Sea: Identifying the Triggers of Expansion," *Naval War College Review*, Vol. 51, No. 2, Spring 1998, available from *www.globalsecurity.org/ military/library/report/1998/art5-sp8.htm*; and Stein Tonnesson, "The Economic Dimension: Natural Resources and Sea Lanes," Timo Kivimaki, ed., *War or Peace in the South China Sea?* Copenhagen, Denmark: Nordic Institute of Asian Studies Press, 2002, p. 56.

24. Wong; and Jane Perlez, "China and Vietnam Point Fingers after Clash in South China Sea," *The New York Times*, May 27, 2014, available from *www.nytimes.com/2014/05/28/world/asia/ vietnam.html?partner=rss&emc=rss&_r=0*.

25. *South China Sea (II)*, ICG, pp. 3, 33; Seth Robson, "China's Tactics Turning Off Asian Neighbors," *Stars and Stripes*, June 25, 2013, available from *www.military.com/daily-news/2013/06/25/ chinas-tactics-turning-off-asian-neighbors.html?ESRC=airforce-a. nl*; and Ronald O. O'Rourke, *Maritime Territorial and Exclusive Economic Zone (EEZ) Disputes Involving China: Issues for Congress,* Washington, DC: Congressional Research Service, August 9, 2013, p. 25, available from *www.fas.org/sgp/crs/row/R42784.pdf*.

26. Irene Chan and Li Mingjiang, "Political Will and Joint Development in the South China Sea" draft document, *Recent Development of the South China Sea Dispute Conference*, Haikou, China, December 2012, p. 9, available from *www.nanhai.org.cn/include_lc/ upload/UploadFiles/20131291011846088.pdf*.

27. Fravel, "Maritime Security in the South China Sea," p. 36. In part, this is because the "involvement of non-claimants in joint exploration in the South China Sea also feeds Beijing's fears of containment," like the pact signed in April 2012 between Russia's Gazprom and PetroVietnam to explore two blocks on the Vietnamese continental shelf, or joint exploration with India's Oil and Natural Gas Company Videsh that may counter China's strong support for Pakistan. *South China Sea (II)*, ICG, pp. 28-29, 33.

28. Hong, p. 186; and Dolven, Kan, and Manyin, p. 21.

29. Douglas H. Paal, "Territorial Disputes in Asian Waters," Washington, DC: Carnegie Endowment for International Peace,

October 16, 2012, available from *carnegieendowment.org/2012/10/16/ territorial-disputes-in-asian-waters/e1ez*; and *South China Sea (II)*, ICG, p. 33.

30. *South China Sea (II)*, ICG, p. 14.

31. *Ibid.*, p. 7.

32. *Ibid.*, p. 38; "South China Sea" Map 737328, Washington DC: CIA, December 1995.

33. Henry Sanderson, "Xi Calls for Boosting China's Navy as Army Marks Anniversary," *Bloomberg News*, August 1, 2013, available from *www.bloomberg.com/news/2013-08-01/xi-calls-for-boosting-china-s-navy-as-military-marks-anniversary.html*.

34. John Boudreau, "China-Vietnam Expand Joint Exploration Deal Amid Tension at Sea," *Bloomberg News*, June 20, 2013, available from *www.bloomberg.com/news/2013-06-20/china-vietnam-expand-joint-exploration-deal-amid-tension-at-sea.html*.

35. Dolven, Kan, and Manyin, p. 20.

36. Hong, p. 57; and *World Factbook*, CIA, "Paracel Islands."

37. Stein Tonnesson, "The History of the Dispute," Timo Kivimaki, ed., *War or Peace in the South China Sea?* Copenhagen, Denmark: Nordic Institute of Asian Studies Press, 2002, p. 7; Pan; and Jon M. Van Dyke and Dale L. Bennett, "Islands and the Delimitation of Ocean Space in the South China Seas," Elisabeth Mann Borgese, Norton Ginsburg, and Joseph R. Morgan, eds., *Ocean Yearbook 10*, Chicago, IL: University of Chicago Press, 1993, p. 65. Even today, the PLAN continues to build fishermen shelters as it has on Money Island and others in the Paracels. Wikipedia, "Money Island," *Wikipedia.org*, undated, available from *en.m.wikipedia. org/wiki/Money_Island,_Paracel_Islands*; and Greenfield, pp. 29-30.

38. Bob Hackett, Sander Kingsepp, and Anthony Tully, "Japanese Occupation South China Sea Islands," *Rising Storm — The Imperial Japanese Navy and China*, 2012, available from *www.combinedfleet.com/SouthChinaSea_t.htm*; Van Dyke and Bennett, pp. 69, 72; Jianming Shen, "Territorial Aspects of the South

China Sea Islands Disputes," Myron H. Nordquist and John Norton Moore, eds., *Security Flashpoints: Oil, Islands, Sea Access and Military Confrontation,* The Hague, The Netherlands: Martinus Nijhoff Publishers, 1998, pp. 173-174, 184; and Mrs. Marie Chung, interview conducted with author in Rockville, MD, August 12, 2013.

39. Guano is an important part of traditionally made fertilizer because it is high in plant-essential nitrogen, phosphate, and potassium content. "Paracel Islands," *The Columbia Electronic Encyclopedia,* 2012, and List of Countries of the World, "Paracel Islands." List of Countries of the World, undated, available from *www.listofcountriesoftheworld.com/pf.html.* A Chinese geologic survey in 1929 reported that Woody Island was particularly rich with guano deposits up to a quarter of a meter deep and estimated at 175,000 tons. The survey observed approximately 48,500 tons of guano had already been removed, presumably by Mitsui Bussan Kaisha or some other company. Chu, pp. 93-94.

40. Ness, p. 43; and Daniel Ten Kate and David Lerman, "Hagel Set for Vietnam Embrace as Wary Asia Eyes Rising China," *Bloomberg News,* May 31, 2013, available from *www.bloomberg.com/news/2013-05-30/hagel-set-for-vietnam-embrace-as-asian-leaders-eye-rising-china.html.*

41. Minnie Chan, "Major Development Plan for Woody Island Unveiled," *South China Morning Post,* November 4, 2012, available from *www.scmp.com/news/china/article/1074996/major-development-plan-woody-island-unveiled. Wikipedia* reports that Woody Island boasts the Xisha Maritime Museum, a Naval Museum, towers erected by the Imperial Japanese Army, a monument erected by ROC forces in 1946, and a PRC monument erected in 1974 as its tourist attractions. Tourists to the Paracels require a special permit to visit. "Woody Island," *Wikipedia.org,* undated, *en.wikipedia.org/wiki/Woody_Island_(South_China_Sea).*

42. K. Oanh Ha, "Vietnam Protests China's Planned Paracel Islands Sailboat Race," *Bloomberg News,* March 30, 2012, available from *www.bloomberg.com/news/2012-03-31/vietnam-protests-china-s-planned-paracel-islands-sailboat-race.html.*

43. Kivimaki, "Conclusion," p. 165.

44. Dodds, p. 14; and Hasjim Djalal, "South China Sea Island Disputes," Myron H. Nordquist and John Norton Moore, eds., *Security Flashpoints: Oil, Islands, Sea Access and Military Confrontation*, The Hague, The Netherlands: Martinus Nijhoff Publishers, 1998, p. 110. Some commentators have speculated that one of China's motivations in seizing the Paracels in 1974 was to forestall such a move by its rival, the Soviet Union, who could turn the islands into a forward operating base against China. No evidence has been found to show that was indeed part of the Chinese decision-making. M. Taylor Fravel, *Strong Borders, Secure Nation: Cooperation and Conflict in China's Territorial Dispute*, Princeton, NJ: Princeton University Press, 2008, pp. 267, 287.

45. The Chinese source does not define what constitutes a "major" attack in his accounting. Thomas G. Mahnken, *Asia in the Balance: Transforming US Military Strategy in Asia*, Washington DC: American Enterprise Institute, May 2012, p. 12, available from *www.aei.org/files/2012/05/31/-asia-in-the-balance-transforming-us-military-strategy-in-asia_134736206767.pdf*; Andrew S. Erikson and Lyle J. Goldstein, "Introduction: In the Same Boat Together," Andrew S. Erickson, Lyle J. Goldstein, and Nan Li, eds., *China, the United States, and 21st Century Sea Power*, Newport, RI: Naval Institute Press, 2010, p. xxi; and David Lai, *The United States and China in Power Transition*, Carlisle, PA: Strategic Studies Institute, U.S. Army War College, December 2011, p. 213.

46. Hackett, Kingsepp, and Tully; and Hong, p. 17,

47. Colin Dueck, "The Return of Geopolitics," Washington, DC: Foreign Policy Research Institute, July 27, 2013, from *www.realclearworld.com/articles/2013/07/27/the_return_of_geo politics_105345.html*; Valencia, Van Dyke, and Ludwig, p. 21; Hong, p. 16; and Shen, p. 173.

48. Hackett, Kingsepp, and Tully; Hong, p. 7; Tonnesson, "History of the Dispute," p. 9; *Nota Bene*; and Shen, p. 177.

49. Hong, p. 10; Tonnesson, "History of the Dispute," p. 10; Hackett, Kingsepp, and Tully; and *World Factbook*, CIA, "Paracel Islands."

50. Van Dyke and Bennett, p. 67; *Nota Bene*; and Hackett, Kingsepp, and Tully. Chinese sources cite a March 30, 1939, Japanese proclamation reporting, "The statements of Great Britain and France made respectively in 1900 and 1921 already declared that the Xisha [Paracel] Islands were a part of the Administrative Prefecture of Hainan Island." Shen, p. 181.

51. Van Ngac Ha, "The January 19, 1974, Naval Battle for the Paracels against the People's Republic of China Navy in the East Sea," Ha Manh Chi, trans., January 2013, available from *vnnavy-dallas.com/tailieu/hoang_sa_01_19_1974.pdf*; Shen, p. 182; Hong, p. 10; Tonnesson, "The History of the Dispute," p. 11; and Van Dyke and Bennett, p. 72.

52. Van Dyke and Bennett, p. 7.

53. Hong, p. 12; *Nota Bene*; and *South China Sea (II)*, ICG, p. 37.

54. Fravel, *Strong Borders, Secure Nation*, pp. 273-274; Tonnesson, "History of the Dispute," p. 11; *Nota Bene*; and Hong, p. 10.

55. *Nota Bene*; Fravel, *Strong Borders, Secure Nation*, p. 274.

56. Fravel, *Strong Borders, Secure Nation*, p. 276; and *Encyclopedia Britannica*, undated, "Paracel Islands," available from *www.britannica.com/EBchecked/topic/442423/Paracel-Islands*.

57. Fravel, *Strong Borders, Secure Nation*, pp. 281, 285-286; and *Nota Bene*.

58. *Encyclopedia Britannica*, "Paracel Islands," and Van Ngac Ha.

59. Fravel, *Strong Borders, Secure Nation*, p. 280.

60. *Ibid.*, pp. 280-282; and *South China Sea (II)*, ICG, pp. 2-3.

61. *South China Sea (II)*, ICG, pp. 2-3; and Fravel, *Strong Borders, Secure Nation*, pp. 280-283.

62. Van Dyke and Bennett, p. 57.

63. For Vietnam, the number killed in this action varies up to 120, and losses are reported between one and three vessels. No reliable numbers of Chinese deaths are confirmed, or if any of its vessels were lost or damaged. Christopher C. Joyner, "The Spratly Islands Dispute: Legal Issues and Prospects for Diplomatic Accommodation," John C. Baker and David G. Wiencek, eds., *Cooperative Monitoring in the South China Sea: Satellite Imagery, Confidence-Building Measures, and the Spratly Islands Disputes*, Westport, CT: Praeger Publishers, 2002; Van Dyke and Bennett, p. 59; Fravel, "Maritime Security in the South China Sea," pp. 35-36; *South China Sea (II)*, ICG, pp. 2-3; Fravel, *Strong Borders, Secure Nation*, pp. 278-279, 290, 295; and Djalal, "South China Seas Island Disputes," p. 117.

64. Casualties and damage from this skirmish are unknown, but both sides retained their islet positions. Studeman.

65. *South China Sea (II)*, ICG, pp. 2-3.

66. David G. Wiencek and John C. Baker, "Security Risks of a South China Sea Conflict," John C. Baker and David G. Wiencek, eds., *Cooperative Monitoring in the South China Sea: Satellite Imagery, Confidence-Building Measures, and the Spratly Islands Disputes*, Westport, CT: Praeger Publishers, 2002.

67. Lai, *The United States and China in Power Transition*, p. 136; and Robert D. Kaplan, "The South China Sea is the Future of Conflict," *Foreign Policy*, Vol. 188, 2011, p. 80. On December 25, 1971, the PRC issued its 497th and final protest over U.S. violations of airspace over the Paracel Islands. Fravel, *Strong Borders, Secure Nation*, p. 279.

68. Rongsheng Ma, "Geostrategic Thinking on Land-and-Sea Integration," *China Military Science Journal*, Vol. 1, No. 1, 2012, p. 58; "China," Washington, DC: U.S. Energy Information Administration (USEIA), September 4, 2012, available from *www.eia.gov/countries/country-data.cfm?fips=CH*; *World Factbook*, CIA, "China"; and Jane Perlez, "Chinese, with Revamped Force, Make Presence Known in East China Sea," *The New York Times*, July 28, 2013, p. A9.

69. Fravel, *Strong Borders, Secure Nation*, p. 300.

70. Gabriel B. Collins, "China's Dependence on the Global Maritime Commons," Andrew S. Erickson, Lyle J. Goldstein, and Nan Li, eds., *China, the United States, and 21st Century Sea Power*, Newport, RI: Naval Institute Press, 2010, p. 21; Peter A. Dutton, "Charting the Course: Sino-American Naval Cooperation to Enhance Governance and Security," Andrew S. Erickson, Lyle J. Goldstein, and Nan Li, eds., *China, the United States, and 21st Century Sea Power*, Newport, RI: Naval Institute Press, 2010, p. 214; Michael D. Swaine and M. Taylor Fravel, "China's Assertive Behavior—Part One: On 'Core Interests'," *China Leadership Monitor*, Vol. 34, Winter 2011, pp. 7-9, available from *www.carnegie endowment.org/files/CLM34MS_FINAL.pdf*; and Kaplan, "The Geography of Chinese Power."

71. John Boudreau, "Vietnam Leader in China Seeks Export Gains Amid Sea Tension," *Bloomberg News*, June 19, 2013, available from *www.bloomberg.com/news/2013-06-19/vietnam-leader-visiting-china-seeks-export-gain-amid-sea-tension.html*; and Kate and Lerman.

72. Fravel, *Strong Borders, Secure Nation*, p. 3.

73. Timo Kivimaki, "Introduction," Timo Kivimaki, ed., *War or Peace in the South China Sea?* Copenhagen, Denmark: Nordic Institute of Asian Studies Press, 2002, p. 1.

74. In comparison, the NATO standard runway length for fighter operations is 2,450-m. Dennis J. Blasko and M. Taylor Fravel, "Much Ado about the Sansha Garrison," *The Diplomat*, August 23, 2012, *thediplomat.com/2012/08/23/much-ado-about-the-sansha-garrison/?all=true*; *World Factbook*, CIA, "Paracel Islands"; and Greenfield, p. 27.

75. D. Collins, "China Counters U.S. Asia-Pivot Strategy. Fortifies Island Military Base," *China Money Report*, August 13, 2012, available from *www.thechinamoneyreport.com/2012/08/13/china-counters-u-s-asia-pivot-strategy-fortifies-island-military-base/*; and Andrei Chang, "Analysis: China's Air-Sea Buildup," *Space War*, September 26, 2008, available from *www.spacewar.com/reports/Analysis_Chinas_air-sea_buildup_999.html*.

76. *World Factbook*, CIA, "Paracel Islands"; Chang; and D. Collins, "China Counters U.S. Asia-Pivot Strategy."

77. Chan; and Blasko and Fravel.

78. Blasko and Fravel. Vietnam refers to the South China Sea as the "East Sea," and the Chinese use the name "South Sea." In 2011, the Philippines began referring to it as the "West Philippine Sea" to reinforce its own claims in the Spratly Islands and undercut that of the Chinese. Dona Pazzibugan and Norman Bordadora, "'It's West Philippine Sea': Gov't, AFP Use It Now to Refer to Disputed Spratly Area," *Philippine Daily Inquirer*, June 11, 2011, available from *newsinfo.inquirer.net/13833/%e2%80%98it%e2%80%99s-west-philippine-sea%e2%80%99.*

79. D. Collins, "China Counters U.S. Asia-Pivot Strategy"; and Blasko and Fravel.

80. Chang.

81. David G. Wiencek and John C. Baker, "Security Risks of a South China Sea Conflict," John C. Baker and David G. Wiencek, eds., *Cooperative Monitoring in the South China Sea: Satellite Imagery, Confidence-Building Measures, and the Spratly Islands Disputes*, Westport, CT: Praeger Publishers, 2002.

82. Chang; Ryan Clarke, *Chinese Energy Security: The Myth of the PLAN's Frontline Status*, Carlisle, PA: Strategic Studies Institute, U.S. Army War College, August 2010, p. vii, available from *www.strategicstudiesinstitute.army.mil/pdffiles/pub1012.pdf*; Elbridge Colby, "Don't Sweat AirSea Battle," *The National Interest*, July 31, 2013, available from *nationalinterest.org/commentary/dont-sweat-airsea-battle-8804*; and Dueck.

83. Blasko and Fravel.

84. Kirk Spitzer, "New Garrison, Old Troubles in the South China Sea," *Time Magazine*, July 26, 2013, available from *nation.time.com/2012/07/26/new-garrison-old-troubles-in-the-south-china-seas/.*

85. Blasko and Fravel; and Spitzer.

86. Fravel, *Strong Borders, Secure Nation*, p. 274.

87. Blasko and Fravel; Fravel, *Strong Borders, Secure Nation*, p. 275; Greenfield, p. 30; and Wanli Yu, "The American Factor in China's Maritime Strategy," Andrew S. Erickson, Lyle J. Goldstein, and Nan Li, eds., *China, the United States, and 21st Century Sea Power*, Newport, RI: Naval Institute Press, 2010, p. 474. Fravel reports that the PLAN completed 76 long-range patrols to both the Amphitrite and Crescent Groups between 1960 and 1973.

88. Robert Sutter and Chin Hao Huang, "China-Southeast Asia Relations: Managing Rising Tension in the South China Sea," *Comparative Connections*, Vol. 13, No. 2, September 2011, p. 67.

89. Studeman; Wiencek and Baker; Van Dyke and Bennett, p. 57; and Hong, p. 74.

90. Fravel, "Maritime Security in the South China Sea," p. 36; and Sutter and Huang, p. 68.

91. "Roiling the Waters: Tensions Rise between China and Vietnam in the South China Sea," *The Economist*, July 7, 2012, available from *www.economist.com/node/21558262*; and Koh.

92. O'Rourke, *Maritime Territorial and EEZ Disputes*, pp. 20-23; and Chan and Li, p. 7.

93. These were sometimes referred to as five "dragons stirring up the sea." The five maritime agencies included: Maritime Police of the Border Control Department (BCD), the largest and only armed agency; Maritime Safety Administration, second largest, under the Ministry of Transportation; Fisheries Law Enforcement Command (FLEC) under the Ministry of Agriculture; General Administration Customs; and the Marine Surveillance Force (MSF) overseeing pollution and science through the State Oceanic Administration. Of these, the FLEC was noted as particularly aggressive. Lyle J. Goldstein, "Improving Chinese Maritime Enforcement Capabilities," Andrew S. Erickson, Lyle J. Goldstein, and Nan Li, eds., *China, the United States, and 21st Century Sea Power*, Newport, RI: Naval Institute Press, 2010, p. 127; Dolven, Kan, and Manyin, pp. 23-24; and Perlez, "Chinese, with Revamped Force," p. A9.

94. This new organization appears to be modeled on the U.S. Coast Guard. Perlez, "Chinese, with Revamped Force," p. A9.

95. Hong, p. 229; Spitzer; *South China Sea (II)*, ICG, p. 28; O'Rourke, *Maritime Territorial and EEZ Disputes*, p. 22; and Chan and Li, pp. 6-7.

96. O'Rourke, *Maritime Territorial and EEZ Disputes*, pp. 20-21; and Sutter and Huang, p. 70.

97. Sutter and Huang, p. 71.

98. In 2011, no Vietnamese fishing ships were detained, although catches and equipment continued to be confiscated, showing how improvement in relations with Vietnam was reflected at sea after the SSRFAB was made to adhere to Foreign Ministry policy. Fravel, "Maritime Security in the South China Sea," p. 45.

99. *South China Sea (II)*, ICG, pp. 4-7; Fravel, "Maritime Security in the South China Sea," p. 38; Hong, p. 31; and Sutter and Huang, p. 67.

100. David Barboza, "China: Vietnam Alleges Attack," *New York Times*, March 27, 2013, p. A6; Boudreau, "China Vietnam Expand Joint Exploration Deal"; John Boudreau, "Vietnam Lodges China Protest over Claims of Attack on Fisherman," *Bloomberg News*, July 18, 2013, available from *www.bloomberg.com/news/2013-07-18/vietnam-lodges-china-protest-over-claims-of-attack-on-fishermen.html*; Associated Press (AP), "Rare Protest in Vietnam Raises a Call to Curb China," *New York Times*, June 3, 2013, p. A7; and Sanderson.

101. O'Rourke, *Maritime Territorial and EEZ Disputes*, p. 27.

102. *Ibid.*, pp. 23-24; and *South China Sea (II)*, ICG, p. ii.

103. Robson.

104. O'Rourke, *Maritime Territorial and EEZ Disputes*, p. 23.

105. Hong, p. 74.

106. Fravel, "Maritime Security in the South China Sea," p. 38.

107. D. Collins, "Fish Wars 2."

108. Hong, p. 21; Studeman; and Bjorn Moller, "The Military Aspects of the Disputes," Timo Kivimaki, ed., *War or Peace in the South China Sea?* Copenhagen, Denmark: Nordic Institute of Asian Studies Press, 2002, p. 77.

109. Dolven, Kan, and Manyin, p. i; *South China Sea (II)*, ICG, p. iii.

110. Djalal, "South China Seas Island Disputes," pp. 111 -112, 116-117.

111. "South China Sea," USEIA. In 2004, 74 percent of Chinese oil imports originated from the Middle East or Africa, and most of that transited the South China Sea enroute to Chinese ports. This number has since grown as the Chinese economy grows with its domestic production levels. Over half of China's oil and over a quarter of its natural gas was imported in 2011. *World Factbook*, CIA, "China"; Daojiong Zha, "China's Energy Security and Its International Relations," *The China and Eurasia Forum Quarterly*, Vol. 3, No. 3, November 2005, p. 49; and Ingolf Kiesow, *China's Quest for Energy: Impact upon Foreign and Security Policy*, Stockholm, Sweden: Swedish Defence Research Agency, November 2004, pp. 12-15.

112. Wiencek and Baker; Pan; Kaplan, "The South China Sea is the Future of Conflict," p. 79; Djalal, "South China Seas Island Disputes," p. 112; and Hong, p. 5. As the world's largest consumer of energy and second largest consumer of oil, China imports 57 percent of its oil and 29 percent of its natural gas, over half of both forms of energy transit the South China Sea. "China," USEIA; and *World Factbook*, CIA, "China."

113. Fravel, "Maritime Security in the South China Sea," p. 35; Greenfield, p. 26; and "South China Sea," Map, CIA.

114. *USPACOM Strategy*, Camp Smith, HI: U.S. Pacific Command, January 22, 2013, p. 2.

115. Baker and Wiencek.

116. Fravel, "Maritime Security in the South China Sea," pp. 33-34; and Kate and Lerman.

117. Van Dyke and Bennett, p. 88; and Shicun Wu, "Opportunities and Challenges for China-US Cooperation in the South China Sea," Andrew S. Erickson, Lyle J. Goldstein, and Nan Li, eds., *China, the United States, and 21st Century Sea Power*, Newport, RI: Naval Institute Press, 2010, p. 368.

118. Robson. Japan, for instance, is militarily able to project naval power into the South China Sea, but is too politically hobbled by its constitution and historical enmity after World War II to play a direct role in the region. See Wiencek and Baker. South Korea's naval force projection is limited and needed closer to home to protect against an erratic North Korea. Taiwan's navy is capable and in close proximity, but in times of increased friction in the region would be needed to defend the homeland, and Taiwan is not diplomatically recognized by any of the other claimant states. The Philippines are militarily weak, and rely heavily on its defense alliance with the United States to maintain its security. Other states, including Vietnam, see the U.S. presence as a counterbalance to a militarily strong and actively involved PRC.

119. Fravel, "Maritime Security in the South China Sea," p. 42; Kaplan, "The South China Sea is the Future of Conflict," pp. 82-83; and Timo Kivimaki, Liselotte Odgaard, and Stein Tonnesson, "What Could be Done?" Timo Kivimaki, ed., *War or Peace in the South China Sea?* Copenhagen, Denmark: Nordic Institute of Asian Studies Press, 2002, p. 141.

120. Robson.

121. Baker and Wiencek; and Roger Baker, "China Tests Japanese and US Patience," Stratfor, February 26, 2013, available from *www.stratfor.com/weekly/china-tests-japanese-and-us-patience?0=ip_login_no_cache%3D0db3ba6f158f595665f79187a45574ed.*

122. Kaplan, "South China Sea is the Future of Conflict"; and Kaplan "The Geography of Chinese Power."

123. Pan; Erikson and Goldstein, p. xiii; and Ronald O. O'Rourke, *China Naval Modernization: Implications for U.S. Navy Capabilities — Background and Issues for Congress,* Washington, DC: Congressional Research Service, December 10, 2012, p. i, available from *www.fas.org/sgp/crs/row/RL33153.pdf.*

124. Valencia, Van Dyke, and Ludwig, p. 2; and Kivimaki, "Introduction," p. 1.

125. David N. Griffiths, "Challenges in the Development of Military-to-Military Relationships," Andrew S. Erickson, Lyle J. Goldstein, and Nan Li, eds., *China, the United States, and 21st Century Sea Power*, Newport, RI: Naval Institute Press, 2010, pp. 38-39.

126. Nerys Avery, "China Streamlines Maritime Law Enforcement Amid Island Disputes," *Bloomberg News,* March 10, 2013. available from *www.bloomberg.com/news/2013-03-10/china-bolsters-maritime-law-enforcement-amid-island-disputes.html*; Spitzer; and Valencia, Van Dyke, and Ludwig, p. 131.

127. Spitzer.

128. O'Rourke, *China Naval Modernization*, p. 8. The ROC and Vietnam also make similarly wide claims to all of the South China Sea, but have not enforced them to the extent that the PRC has.

129. Dolven, Kan, and Manyin, p. 5.

130. Fravel, *Strong Borders, Secure Nation*, p. 275.

131. Peter J. Brown, "US and China Can't Calm South China Sea," *Asia Times,* June 4, 2010. available from *www.atimes.com/atimes/China/LF04Ad01.html.*

132. O'Rourke, *China Naval Modernization,* p. 8; *South China Sea (II),* ICG, p. 18; and O'Rourke, *Maritime Territorial and EEZ Disputes,* p. 4.

133. Lai, *The United States and China in Power Transition,* p. 120; Hong, p. 32; and O'Rourke, *China Naval Modernization,* p. 8.

134. *South China Sea,* ICG, p. 18; Fravel, "Maritime Security in the South China Sea," p. 35; and Hong, pp. 30-31.

135. Matthew Lee, "US Takes Aim at China, Ups Naval Aid to SE Asia," *Associated Press,* December 16, 2013, available from *news.yahoo.com/us-takes-aim-china-ups-naval-aid-se-105727402--politics.html.*

136. Hong, pp. 93-94.

137. Fravel, "Maritime Security in the South China Sea," p. 34; and Ivan Shearer, "Navigation Issues in the Asian Pacific Region," James Crawford and D. R. Rothwell, *The Law of the Sea in the Asian Pacific Region,* Boston, MA: Martinus Nijhoff Publishers, 1995, p. 219.

138. Valencia, Van Dyke, and Ludwig, p. 17; and Hong, p. 58.

139. Hong, p. 222.

140. *Ibid.,* p. 93.

141. *Ibid.,* p. 223; and Van Dyke and Bennett, p. 89.

142. Joyner.

143. Hong, pp. 42, 54-55.

144. Or more like adding apples and oranges. Since the imposition of the Treaty Port System in 1842, however, Asian societies have had to assimilate European-imposed international customary law in order to compete successfully to retain or gain land. Van Dyke and Bennett, pp. 62-63; and Kivimaki, "Conclusion," p. 126.

145. Hong, pp. 109-110.

146. *South China Sea (II),* ICG, p. 29.

147. Hong, p. 54; and Shicun Wu, p. 365.

148. Kivimaki, Odgaard, and Tonnesson, p. 154.

149. In 1962, the International Law Commission outlined the criteria for exercising authority over an historic area as the continuous exercise of that authority and repeated use of the area, and acceptance of these by other states in *Juridical Regime of Historic Waters, Including Historic Bays*. Valencia, Van Dyke, and Ludwig, p. 26; Van Dyke and Bennett, p. 80; and Shearer, p. 208. Part of the confusion with use of these terms by the Chinese is that its media and education system imprecisely use them as broad-sweeping terms that builds the public's nationalist expectations and muddies any reasoned debate over these issues. Chan and Li, p. 8.

150. Hong, p. 66, and Valencia, Van Dyke, and Ludwig, p. 26.

151. Hong, p. 16; and Lai, *The United States and China in Power Transition*, pp. 127-128.

152. Valencia, Van Dyke, and Ludwig, p. 66; and Hong, pp. 66, 70-71.

153. Sutter and Huang, p. 71; and Hong, pp. 63, 130.

154. Valencia, Van Dyke, and Ludwig, p. 25; and Hong, pp. 64-65.

155. *South China Sea (II)*, ICG, p. 29.

156. Wiencek and Baker.

157. Despite their many other disagreements, the PRC and ROC both assert identical historic and other claims to the South China Sea based on the same historic evidence, as fully described later in this section.

158. "South China Sea," USEIA; Hong, p. 17; *South China Sea (II)*, ICG, p. 37; Shen, p. 141.

159. Valencia, Van Dyke, and Ludwig, p. 30; and Van Ngac Ha.

160. Van Dyke and Bennett, p. 68; and Valencia, Van Dyke, and Ludwig, p. 30.

161. Greenfield, pp. 26-27; Van Dyke and Bennett, p. 69; and Hong, pp. 6-7.

162. Shicun Wu, p. 366.

163. *South China Sea (II)*, ICG, p. 37; Hong, p. 17; Tonnesson, "History of the Dispute," p. 12; Van Dyke and Bennett, p. 72; and Shicun Wu, p. 365.

164. Hong, p. 69.

165. Dr. David Lai, interview on February 21, 2013 at Carlisle Barracks, PA.

166. Hong pp. 6-7; Shen, pp. 143-144; and Tonnenson, "The History of the Dispute," p. 8.

167. Hong, p. 12; and Valencia, Van Dyke, and Ludwig, p. 21.

168. North Vietnam was known as the Democratic Republic of Vietnam (DRV) until 1976, and after reunification the communist government renamed itself the Socialist Republic of Vietnam (SRV).

169. Tonnenson, "The History of the Dispute," p. 16; and Fravel, *Strong Borders, Secure Nation*, p. 286; Hong, p. 17; and Shen, pp. 142-143.

170. Fravel, *Strong Borders, Secure Nation*, p. 269.

171. *Nota Bene.* The transfer of White Dragon Tail Island (Dao Bach Long Vi) is the only maritime transfer of sovereignty ever made by the PRC. That is why some analysts suspect a deal was made for tacit recognition of Chinese sovereignty in the Paracels and Spratlys, but it may have also been meant to support fellow-communist North Vietnam in its conflict with South Vietnam and external powers. Fravel, *Strong Borders, Secure Nation*, pp. 268-269. On the other hand, the PRC has compromised dozens of times in finalizing land border deals with neighbors. For an excellent

analysis of the PRC's land border settlement treaties, see M. Taylor Fravel's *Strong Borders, Secure Nation: Cooperation and Conflict in China's Territorial Disputes.*

172. Although Vietnam, the PRC, and the ROC all claim the Paracel and Spratly Islands in their entirety (along with Malaysia, the Philippines, and Brunei, which claim parts or all of the Spratleys), Vietnam does not claim Macclesfield Bank or Scarborough Shoal, which lie further to the east or north of those island groups. The Philippines, however, does dispute both of these geologic features with China. Lai, *The United States and China in Power Transition*, p. 131.

173. Valencia, Van Dyke, and Ludwig, p. 25; Sutter and Huang, p. 71; USEIA, "South China Sea"; Lai, *The United States and China in Power Transition*, p. 222; Djalal, "South China Seas Island Disputes," p. 113; Shen, p. 140; and Dolven, Kan, and Manyin, pp. 6, 8.

174. The Chinese claim was originally drawn with 11-dashed lines, but revised to 9-dashed lines in 1953 when two were removed in the Gulf of Tonkin without explanation. Some observers feel that the use of a dashed line rather than a solid one also indicates the claim is subject to change, and China and Vietnam have bilaterally negotiated a partial maritime border in the Gulf of Tonkin in 2000. Brown; *South China Sea (II)*, ICG, p. 36; Fravel, "Maritime Security in the South China Sea," pp. 41-42; "Maritime Claims of Northeast Asia" Map, CIA; and Dolven, Kan, and Manyin, p. 8. In 2012, a PRC foreign ministry spokesperson may have indicated some clarification in stating, "No country including China has claimed sovereignty over the entire South China Sea," and that China's claims in the 9-dashed line were for land features and not to the entire water area. *South China Sea (II)*, ICG, p. 4. Promising though such a statement seems for transparency, internal rifts within the government may "clarify" the position differently later continuing the ambiguity to its claim. Although diplomatically useful, in negotiations a vague claim may weaken its legal status, since historic claims should be well known and understood by other countries in order for them to be recognized as Chinese. Valencia, Van Dyke, and Ludwig, p. 27.

175. Joyner; Shen, p. 139; and Ramses Amer, "Claims and Conflict Situations," Timo Kivimaki, ed., *War or Peace in the South China Sea?* Copenhagen, Denmark: Nordic Institute of Asian Studies Press, 2002, p. 34.

176. Joyner; and Fravel, *Strong Borders, Secure Nation,* p. 268.

177. *South China Sea (II)*, ICG, p. 1; Sutter and Huang, p. 70; and Dolven, Kan, and Manyin, p. 10.

178. "South China Sea," USEIA; Greenfield, pp. 21-22; Sutter and Huang, p. 71; Shen, p. 149; and Hong, p. 16.

179. Greenfield, p. 31; Van Dyke and Bennett, pp. 62-63; and Shen, p. 165. For a more detailed listing of Chinese historic references, see Shicun Wu, pp. 22-34, and Jianming Shen, pp. 139-218.

180. Valencia, Van Dyke, and Ludwig, p. 21; Hong, p. 16; and Shen, p. 173.

181. Chu, p. 91; Valencia, Van Dyke, and Ludwig, pp. 22-24.

182. Hong, p. 101. It is worth noting that the present *Law of the Sea Treaty* categorizes islands as above the water at high tide, not the low water tide method cited here by the Chinese. Hong, p. 50.

183. Sutter and Huang, p. 71; and Greenfield, p. 32.

184. Hong, p. 68; *South China Sea (II)*, ICG, p. 36; and Kaplan, "The South China Sea is the Future of Conflict," pp. 79-80.

185. Greenfield, p. 32; Van Dyke and Bennett, pp. 63-64; "South China Sea," USEIA; and Hong, p. 16.

186. Hong, p. 10.

187. Fravel, "Maritime Security in the South China Sea," p. 41.

188. Hong, p. 68; "South China Sea," USEIA; and *South China Sea (II)*, ICG, p. 36. This area of common interest has offered interesting opportunities for both sides to work together, including joint oceanographic expeditions, economic development schemes,

and the only representation by both parties in multilateral nego-tiations, the Indonesian sponsored Track II talks which include each of the South China Sea claimants. Taiwanese participation in international fora is otherwise proscribed under the PRC's "one China policy." Sutter and Huang, p. 70; Hong, p. 211; Tonnesson, "The History of the Dispute," p. 19; Valencia, Van Dyke, and Lud-wig, p. 96; and *South China Sea (II)*, ICG, p. 12.

189. Greenfield, pp. 29-30; and Tonnesson, "The History of the Dispute," p. 7.

190. "Vietnam Refuses to Stamp New Chinese Passport," AFP, November 27, 2012, available from *www.thenewage.co.za/71785-1020-53-Vietnam_refuses_to_stamp_new_Chinese_passport;* and Sut-ter and Huang, p. 68.

191. Van Dyke and Bennett, pp. 62-63.

192. Valencia, Van Dyke, and Ludwig, pp. 22-24; and Hong, pp. 16, 64.

193. Lai, *The United States and China in Power Transition,* pp. 129, 221.

194. Robson.

195. Valencia, Van Dyke, and Ludwig, pp. 26-27; Hong, p. 70; and Lai, *The United States and China in Power Transition,* p. 140.

196. Hong, pp. 68-69, 116.

197. Valencia, Van Dyke, and Ludwig, p. 39.

198. The Netherlands, on behalf of its colony the Dutch East Indies (today Indonesia), and the United States for its posses-sion of the Philippines, disputed the status of this Philippine Sea island just southeast of Mindanao. The United States based its claimed sovereignty in terms of discovery (inchoate title), while the Netherlands argued and won based on occupation and ef-fective administration (prescriptive occupation). This case estab-lished a long-standing principle that occupation takes precedence over discovery and historic claims. Later rulings by the Interna-

tional Court of Justice in 1953 in the Minquiers and Echreos Case between Great Britain and France over two groups of islets by Jersey, and the Gulf of Fonseca Case by the same court in 1992 that awarded El Tigre Island to Honduras, are based on the same principle. Valencia, Van Dyke, and Ludwig, p. 17.

199. Lai, *The United States and China in Power Transition*, p. 221.

200. Valencia, Van Dyke, and Ludwig, pp. 28, 39; and *South China Sea (II)*, ICG, p. 30.

201. Valencia, Van Dyke, and Ludwig, p. 37; and Hong, p. 16.

202. "Res Nullius Law & Legal Definition," *USLegal*, undated, available from *definitions.uslegal.com/r/res-nullius/*. *Res nullis* may be equated to property without an owner because it is abandoned, which is slightly different from another Latin term also derived from Roman law, *terra nullis* ("land belonging to no one"). *Terra nullis i*s land without an owner because it is newly discovered, "has never been subject to the sovereignty of any state, or over which any prior sovereign has expressly or implicitly relinquished sovereignty." "Terra Nullius Law & Legal Definition," *USLegal*, undated, *definitions.uslegal.com/t/terra-nullius/*. Through *res nullis*, property that is previously known, and perhaps once claimed or occupied but subsequently not in use or abandoned, can be claimed and occupied to establish sovereignty over that land. This monograph uses the term *res nullis* for the status of the Paracel Islands when that claim is made by one of the powers involved. In terms of establishing sovereignty, there is little difference between a feature being occupied using one form or the other, as long as the occupation is effective.

203. Joyner; and Valencia, Van Dyke, and Ludwig, pp. 19-20.

204. They interpret all earlier historic and occupation claims to the South China Sea islands as void because, based on the 1951 San Francisco Treaty, the island group was "de facto under the trusteeship of the Allied Powers" and thus "as 'trusts' nullified any previous ownership of them. . . ." *South China Sea (II)*, ICG, p. 37; Hong, p. 18; and Valencia, Van Dyke, and Ludwig, p. 33, 35.

205. Lai, *The United States and China in Power Transition*, pp. 130-131; and Dolven, Kan, and Manyin, p. 7.

206. Greenfield, pp. 29-30.

207. Hong, p. 10; Tonnesson, "History of the Dispute," p. 11; and Van Dyke and Bennett, pp. 64-65.

208. Van Dyke and Bennett, p. 64; and Hong, p. 10.

209. *Nota Bene*; and Hackett, Kingsepp, and Tully.

210. Hong, p. 10; *Nota Bene*; Amer, "Claims and Conflict Situations," pp. 27-28; and Fravel, "Maritime Security in the South China Sea," p. 41.

211. Fravel, *Strong Borders, Secure Nation*, p. 269.

212. *Ibid.*, pp. 277-278; *Nota Bene*.

213. Fravel, "Maritime Security in the South China Sea," p. 41.

214. *Wikipedia*, "Woody Island."

215. "Q&A: South China Sea Dispute," *BBC News Asia*, January 22, 2013, available from *www.bbc.co.uk/news/world-asia-pacific-13748349*; Dolven, Kan, and Manyin, p. 33; and Blasko and Fravel.

216. Wiencek and Baker; Valencia, Van Dyke, and Ludwig, p. 41; Amer, "Claims and Conflict Situations," p. 28; and Djalal, "South China Seas Island Disputes," p. 131.

217. Hong, p. 10; and Van Dyke and Bennett, p. 72.

218. Fravel, *Strong Borders, Secure Nation,* p. 277; and Greenfield, pp. 32-33.

219. "Da Nang," *Wikipedia.org*, undated, available from *en.wikipedia.org/wiki/Da_Nang*.

220. "Roiling the Waters," p. 39; and Dolven, Kan, and Manyin, p. 11.

221. "Roiling the Waters," p. 39; Spitzer; *South China Sea (II)*, ICG, p. 5; Douglas H Paal, "Dangerous Shoals: US Policy in the South China Sea," Washington, DC: Carnegie Endowment for International Peace, August 11, 2012, available from *carnegieendowment.org/2012/08/11/dangerous-shoals-u.s.-policy-in-south-china-sea/dc0c*; and "Q&A: South China Sea Dispute." China complains that this step of creating an administrative district over its South China Sea claims only follows those of Vietnam and the Philippines, and is unfairly being condemned for its actions. Paal, "Dangerous Shoals."

222. Hong, p. 17; Valencia, Van Dyke, and Ludwig, p. 33; and Greenfield, p. 40.

223. Shen, pp. 177-179.

224. Greenfield, p. 33; and Djalal, "South China Seas Island Disputes," pp. 114-115.

225. Valencia, Van Dyke, and Ludwig, p. 17; and Lai, *The United States and China in Power Transition*, p. 221.

226. "*Uti Possidetis* Law & Legal Definition," *USLegal*, undated, available from *definitions.uslegal.com/u/uti-possidetis/*; and "*Uti Possidetis*," *Wikipedia.org*, undated, available from *en.wikipedia.org/wiki/Uti_possidetis*.

227. Lai, *The United States and China in Power Transition*, p. 140.

228. Stein Tonnesson, "Geopolitics and Maritime Territorial Disputes in East Asia, *Contemporary Southeast Asia*, Vol. 32, No. 1, April 2010, p. 111.

229. Sam Bateman, "Good Order at Sea in the South China Sea," Shicun Wu and Keyuan Zou, eds., *Maritime Security in the South China Sea: Regional Implication and International Cooperation*, Surrey, UK: Ashgate Publishing Limited, 2009, p. 29.

230. Anthony Bergin, "The High Seas Regime—Pacific Trends and Developments," J. Crawford and D. R. Rothwell, eds., *The Law of the Sea in the Asia Pacific Region*, Boston, MA: Martinus Nijhoff Publishers, 1995, pp. 183-185.

231. Bateman, "Good Order at Sea in the South China Sea," p. 29.

232. Hong, pp. 46, 95; and Dolven, Kan, and Manyin, p. 31.

233. Christine Chinkin, "Dispute Resolution and the *Law of the Sea*: Regional Problems and Prospects," J. Crawford and D. R. Rothwell, eds., *The Law of the Sea in the Asia Pacific Region*, Boston, MA: Martinus Nijhoff Publishers, 1995, p. 248; and Shearer, p. 200.

234. Hong, pp. 43-46, 72; and UNCLOS *Declarations and Statements,* New York: UN Division for Ocean Affairs and the *Law of the Sea*, April 10, 2013, "China," available from *www.un.org/depts/los/convention_agreements/convention_declarations.htm*.

235. *South China Sea (II)*, ICG, p. 29.

236. Bergin, p. 195.

237. *United Nations Convention on the Law of the Sea*, New York: UN Division for Ocean Affairs and the *Law of the Sea*, December 10, 1982, p. 63.

238. Hong, p. 51.

239. This number discounts the features in the Macclesfield Bank, about 125-nm further to the southeast, which the *Gazetteer* classifies as part of the Paracel Islands but has been treated by the South China Sea disputants as a separate grouping. Of these 18 features listed in the *Gazetteer*, three (Pyramid Rock, Passau Keah, and Tung Tao) are not assigned territorial water jurisdictions on the CIA's "South China Sea" map, and more data is needed to verify their actual classification. USDMA, *Gazetteer of the Paracel Islands*; and "South China Sea," CIA, Map.

240. Valencia, Van Dyke, and Ludwig, p. 40; and Bergin, p. 196.

241. There are 10 of these geologic features named in the *Gazetteer* as part of the Paracels that would probably not meet territorial waters criteria because they are reefs, banks, atolls, or

other protrusions from the seabed, and many more unnamed features that do not merit such consideration. *Gazetteer of the Paracel Islands.*

242. From *Advisory Opinion on Western Sahara,* 1975. Valencia, Van Dyke, and Ludwig, p. 61.

243. Hong, p. 52; and Van Dyke and Bennett, p. 78.

244. Bergin, p. 196.

245. Valencia, Van Dyke, and Ludwig, pp. 41-42; and Van Dyke and Bennett, p. 89.

246. Valencia, Van Dyke, and Ludwig, p. 43; and Van Dyke and Bennett, pp. 78-79.

247. Van Dyke and Bennett, p. 75.

248. Hong, pp. 51-52; Greenfield, p. 38; and Van Dyke and Bennett, p. 79.

249. Van Dyke and Bennett, pp. 81, 84-85. In 1978, for instance, the International Court of Justice awarded the Isles of Scilly, consisting of six small inhabited British islands in a group of 48 off the coast of Cornwall, only half of their jurisdiction against the maritime zones of France's Brittany Peninsula — deemed the "half effect." This concept was derived from an earlier negotiated settlement between Italy and Yugoslavia. Van Dyke and Bennett, p. 82.

250. These decisions were formed through the International Court of Justice rulings in Tunisia-Libya Continental Shelf Case in 1982. The islands were given circular enclaves of 12-nm territorial water, and the rest of the surrounding maritime zone went to the continental state. Van Dyke and Bennett, pp. 83-86.

251. *Ibid.,* pp. 77, 86; and Hong, p 243.

252. Chu, pp. 92-93; and "Paracel Islands," *Encyclopedia Britannica,* undated, available from *www.britannica.com/EBchecked/topic/442423/Paracel-Islands.*

253. Van Dyke and Bennett, p. 89; Chan; and Spitzer.

254. Dolven, Kan, and Manyin, p. 33; and Chan.

255. Van Dyke and Bennett, pp. 78-79.

256. Hong, p. 59; and Greenfield, p. 38.

257. Valencia, Van Dyke, and Ludwig, p. 56; and Djalal, "South China Seas Island Disputes," p. 125.

258. Dutton, p. 204; and UNCLOS, UN, p. 70.

259. The bay can be no wider than 24-nm between its entrance points. The line connecting the two entrance points becomes the territorial straight baseline. UNCLOS, UN, p. 28; and Shearer, p. 208.

260. UNCLOS, UN, p. 28.

261. At their widest distance from their mainland shores, Vietnam claims 75-nm for its straight baseline point at Isles Catwick (point 6, Hon Hai Islet) and 70-nm southeast of Zhangjiang for China (between declared straight baseline point 31, Dafanshi, and point 32, Qizhouliedao). "Maritime Claims of Northeast Asia," Map, CIA; "South China Sea" Map, CIA; Jin-Hyun Paik, "East Asia and the *Law of the Sea*," James Crawford and D. R. Rothwell, eds., *The Law of the Sea in the Asian Pacific Region*, Boston, MA: Martinus Nijhoff Publishers, 1995, p. 8; Tonnesson, "History of the Dispute," p. 15; Hong, pp. 13, 51, 127, 130-131; and *DoD 2005.1-M, Maritime Claims Reference Manual*, Washington DC: Under Secretary of Defense for Policy, DoD, June 23, 2005, pp. 126, 131, 689-691, available from *www.jag.navy.mil/ organization/documents/mcrm/vietnam.pdf*. See an entire analysis of China's baselines in the USDOS "Straight Baselines Claim: China," and for Vietnam: USDOS, "Straight Baselines Claim: Vietnam," *Limits in the Seas* No. 99, Washington DC: Bureau of Oceans and International Environmental and Scientific Affairs, Department of State, December 12, 1983, available from *www.state.gov/ documents/organization/58573.pdf*.

262. UNCLOS, UN, p. 28.

263. Djalal, "South China Sea Island Disputes."

264. Valencia, Van Dyke, and Ludwig, p. 26.

265. UNCLOS, UN, pp. 40-43; and Joyner.

266. UNCLOS, UN, p. 40; and Shearer, p. 204.

267. Vietnam would also not be eligible to draw archipelagic baselines around the Paracels if it were given sovereignty. UNCLOS, UN, p. 40; and "Straight Baselines Claim: China," Department of State, p. 8.

268. There is no specific maximum length for a straight baseline in UNCLOS, but several analysts place it between 24-nm (the stated limit allowed across the mouth of a bay) to 48-nm (twice that amount). The U.S. Government position is that the maximum baseline length is 24-nm. In its 1996 declaration of its baselines when ratifying UNCLOS, China seems to have misapplied Article 47 rules to the Paracels since the longest baselines measure 79, 76, 41, 36, and 28-nm. While these would be inside the archipelagic baseline rules, the land to water ratio requirement between 1 to 1 and 1 to 9 within those lines are not met. "Straight Baselines Claim China," Department of State, pp. 4-5, 16; "Maritime Claims of Northeast Asia" Map, CIA; Hong Thao Nguyen, "Sovereignty over Paracel and Spratly Archipelagoes," *Thanh Nien Daily*, April 14, 2013, available from *southeastasiansea.wordpress.com/2013/04/13/international-law-and-sovereignty-over-the-paracel-and-spratly-archipelagoes-part-16/*; People's Republic of China, "Declaration of the Government of the People's Republic of China on the Baselines of the Territorial Sea of the People's Republic of China," Beijing, China: Foreign Ministry, May 15, 1996, available from *www.un.org/depts/los/LEGISLATIONANDTREATIES/PDFFILES/DEPOSIT/chn_mzn7_1996.pdf*; Greenfield, pp. 37-38; and UNCLOS, UN, pp. 40-41.

269. UNCLOS, UN, pp. 29-30.

270. Hong, p. 62.

271. Shearer, p. 208; and Valencia, Van Dyke, and Ludwig, p. 28.

272. Shearer, p. 208; and Hong, pp. 64-65.

273. Hong, pp. 60, 64, 67; and *South China Sea (II)*, ICG, pp. 29-30.

274. Hong, p. 71.

275. Valencia, Van Dyke, and Ludwig, p. 28.

276. *South China Sea (II)*, ICG, p. 36. The Chair of the Research, Development and Evaluation Commission of Taiwan's executive branch (*Yuan*) had a different view in 1997 when he observed that the maritime area within the U-line "is the ROC's historical waters, which, although it does not have the status of internal waters, is analogous to archipelagic waters under the 1982 UN-CLOS." Valencia, Van Dyke, and Ludwig, p. 66.

277. Amer, "Claims and Conflict Situations," pp. 30-31.

278. UNCLOS, UN, pp. 35, 66; Valencia, Van Dyke, and Ludwig, p. 47; and *DoD Manual 2005.1*, pp. 126-127, 698.

279. Joyner; Dutton, pp. 202-203; and Shicun Wu and Keyuan Zou, "Maritime Security in the South China Sea: Cooperation and Implications," Shicun Wu and Keyuan Zou, eds., *Maritime Security in the South China Sea: Regional Implication and International Cooperation*, Surrey, UK: Ashgate Publishing Limited, 2009, p. 5.

280. UNCLOS, UN, p. 31; and Hong, p. 72.

281. UNCLOS, UN, p. 33; and Shearer, p. 211.

282. UNCLOS, UN, p. 35; Dutton, p. 203; and Wu and Zou, pp. 4-5.

283. Paik, p. 12; and Shearer, p. 206.

284. UNCLOS, UN, p. 30.

285. Dutton, pp. 210-211; "South China Seas," USEIA; and Shearer, p. 211.

286. Hong, p. 132; and Dolven, Kan, and Manyin, p. 32.

287. Paik, p. 10; and Hong, p. 128.

288. Erikson and Goldstein, p xvii; Guifang Xue, "China and the *Law of the Sea: A Sino-US Maritime Cooperation Perspective*," Andrew S. Erickson, Lyle J. Goldstein, and Nan Li, eds., *China, the United States, and 21st Century Sea Power*, Newport, RI: Naval Institute Press, 2010, p. 176; and Dutton, p. 211.

289. Paik, p. 11; Greenfield, p. 30; Xue, p. 177; and Wiencek and Baker.

290. Hong, p. 114; Xue, p. 176; and UNCLOS *Declarations and Statements*, UN, China Article 4.

291. Hong, p. 110. Coexistence is the Chinese method to order international affairs that requires "extensive policy coordination for conflict management and promotes a system of co-management of global security issues between great powers that subscribe to different programs of international order." Coexistence advocates principles like absolute sovereignty and nonintervention in other states, while the U.S. vision of closer international integration champions principles like economic globalization and recognition of basic human rights. Liselotte Odgaard, "Between Integration and Coexistence US-Chinese Strategies of International Order," *Strategic Studies Quarterly*, Vol. 17, No. 1, Spring 2013, pp. 18-19.

292. Wiencek and Baker; Studeman; and Swaine and Fravel, "China's Assertive Behavior—Part One: On 'Core Interests'," p. 7.

293. UNCLOS, UN, pp. 43-44.

294. Dutton, p. 203; UNCLOS, UN, pp. 43-44; and Wu and Zou, p. 5.

295. Shearer, p. 221; and UNCLOS, UN, pp. 44-49.

296. Shicun Wu, p. 366; and Bateman, "Good Order at Sea in the South China Sea," p. 29.

297. Davor Vidas, "The UN Convention on the *Law of the Sea*, the European Union, and the Rule of Law," Sanford Silverburg, ed., *International Law*, Boulder, CO: Westview Press, 2011, p. 340.

298. *1958 Geneva Conventions on the Law of the Sea*, Geneva, Switzerland: U.N. International Law Commission, April 29, 1958, p. 316, available from *untreaty.un.org/cod/avl/ha/gclos/gclos.html*; and Valencia, Van Dyke, and Ludwig, pp. 49-50.

299. Valencia, Van Dyke, and Ludwig, p. 135.

300. Hong, p. 60. The decision by the International Court of Justice awarding Britain's Channel Islands only territorial waters against the consideration of an entire EEZ to nearby continental France, and the St Pierre et Miquelon case awarding the EEZ to Canada and not the tiny French possessions off its coast. Hong, p. 60; and Van Dyke and Bennett, p. 82.

301. Valencia, Van Dyke, and Ludwig, pp. 50-51, 134.

302. Greenfield, p. 36; Valencia, Van Dyke, and Ludwig, pp. 38; and Hong, p. 20.

303. Valencia, Van Dyke, and Ludwig, p. 48.

304. Valencia, Van Dyke, and Ludwig, p. 31; Greenfield, p. 32; *2012 World Factbook*, CIA, "China," "Vietnam"; and "South China Sea" Map, CIA. Although the Chinese claim is from an island, some scholars have asserted that the Hainan Dao coast would have near equal weighting with Vietnam's continental coastline when overlap is delimited using the equitable principle based on the ICJ's 1969 *North Sea Continental Shelf* cases. Greenfield, p. 34.

305. Valencia, Van Dyke, and Ludwig, p. 31; SRV, "Executive Summary," p. 5; and *South China Sea (II)*, ICG, p. 29.

306. Valencia, Van Dyke, and Ludwig, pp. 55, 146, 257; UNCLOS, UN, p. 57; Hong, p. 59; and "South China Sea" Map, CIA.

307. SRV, "Executive Summary," cover page.

308. "South China Sea" Map, CIA; Hong, p. 60; and Valencia, Van Dyke, and Ludwig, p. 53. Woody Island is hemmed in by the influence of the EEZs from surrounding Hainan Dao to the northwest, Pratas Island to the northeast, and the Vietnamese coast to the south and southwest. Valencia, Van Dyke, and Ludwig, p. 50.

309. The Macclesfield Bank region lies within a 200-m isobath depth. Valencia, Van Dyke, and Ludwig, p. 268. The 40,000 square-nm area was calculated from a sector of a circle centered on Woody Island radiating toward the edge of the high seas to its northeast, as marked 200-nm from ROC-occupied Paratas Island, along an arc nearly due south to the edge of the high seas with Vietnam's coastal EEZ east of Qui Nohn. The smaller sector of China's EEZ generated from Hainan Dao within this wedge was removed, as was a corner of the sector that fell within the Pratas Island-generated EEZ. "South China Sea" Map, CIA. For a map showing the possible South China Sea maritime jurisdiction with a Paracel Islands EEZ, see Plate 12 in Valencia, Van Dyke, and Ludwig, p. 265.

310. Hong, pp. 73, 137.

311. The Crestone Block is now known as the Benton Block. The block straddles Vietnam's EEZ if it is measured from the normal baseline along the coast, but is entirely within Vietnam's delimited EEZ when measured from its disputed straight baseline, which is about 70-nm from the shoreline in this vicinity. This is an example of the advantage gained, and problems raised, with liberal use of straight baselines. "South China Sea" Map, CIA; Valencia, Van Dyke, and Ludwig, p. 27; Studeman; Tonnesson, "The Economic Dimension," p. 56; and "Roiling the Waters," p. 39.

312. Chan and Li, p. 10.

313. Hong, pp. 65, 70; and SRV, "Executive Summary," p. 5.

314. People's Republic of China, *Exclusive Economic Zone and Continental Shelf Act,* Beijing, China: Standing Committee of the Ninth National People's Congress, June 26, 1998, Article 12, available from *www.un.org/Depts/los/LEGISLATIONANDTREATIES/*

PDFFILES/chn_1998_eez_act.pdf; Republic of China, *Law on the Exclusive Economic Zone and the Continental Shelf of the Republic of China,* Taipei, Republic of China: Government of the Republic of China, January 21, 1998, Article 4, available from *en.wikisource. org/wiki/Law_on_the_Exclusive_Economic_Zone_and_the_Continental_Shelf_of_the_Republic_of_China*; and Hong, p. 88.

315. Dolven, Kan, and Manyin, p. 32; Fravel, "Maritime Security in the South China Sea," p. 35; Dutton, p. 210; Xue, p. 193; O'Rourke, *China Naval Modernization,* pp. i, 8; and O'Rourke, *Maritime Territorial and EEZ Disputes,* "Executive Summary."

316. This clause covers the special case of passage through straits, but is also found in Article 19 on innocent passage through territorial waters, and Article 301 on peaceful uses of the seas. UN, UNCLOS, pp. 31, 37, 138; and Dutton, p. 211.

317. Lai, *The United States and China in Power Transition,* p. 121; O'Rourke, *China Naval Modernization,* p. 5; and Xue, p. 181.

318. UNCLOS, UN, p. 44; Dutton, p. 212; and Yongming Jin, "How to Resolve the South China Sea Issue," *China Daily,* July 7, 2011, available from *www.chinadaily.com.cn/cndy/2011-07/07/ content_12850748.htm.*

319. UNCLOS, UN, p. 44; and Dutton, p. 212.

320. There were 27 countries reported by the Congressional Research Service. Lai states 14 countries ban foreign militaries from their EEZs, O'Rourke cites a study of 18, and Dolven, Kan, and Manyin cite 26 countries but state that Vietnam has relaxed its previous requirement from approval to notification. O'Rourke, "Maritime Territorial and EEZ Disputes," p. 4; Lai, *The United States and China in Power Transition,* p. 121; Dolven, Kan, and Manyin, p. 32; and "South China Sea," USEIA. In June 2011,Taiwan's Foreign Ministry seemed to emphasize its support for the U.S. position on the principle of freedom of navigation in a press release. Sutter and Huang, p. 70.

321. Hong, p. 89; Dutton, p. 210; Brown; and Xue, pp. 181, 184.

322. Dutton, p. 215.

323. Greenfield, p. 36; and Valencia, Van Dyke, and Ludwig, p. 24.

324. Timo Koivurova, "Power Politics or Orderly Development?" Sanford Silverburg, ed., *International Law*, Boulder, CO: Westview Press, 2011, p. 365; *1958 Geneva Conventions on the Law of the Sea*, UN, p. 312; and Chan and Li, pp. 2-3.

325. Adjudicated in the North Sea Continental Shelf cases. This decision sparked the need for the third UN Conference on the Law of the Sea starting in 1973, producing the current version of the Law of the Sea Treaty in 1982. Tonnesson, "History of the Dispute," p. 14; and Van Dyke and Bennett, p. 81.

326. Koivurova, pp. 364-365; and Tonnesson, "History of the Dispute," p. 14. Although UNCLOS refers to this region as the continental shelf, in geographic terms it is the continental margin which consists of the relatively flat and shallow continental shelf and the continental slope that drops to the deeper ocean floor. This distinction is relevant because the two defining factors for the extent of the legal continental shelf (the term this monograph will use in accord with UNCLOS) are "either shall not exceed 350 nautical miles from the baselines from which the breadth of the territorial sea is measured or shall not exceed 100 nautical miles from the 2,500 meter isobath, which is a line connecting the depth of 2,500 meters." UNCLOS, UN, p. 53.

327. Valencia, Van Dyke, and Ludwig, p. 37.

328. UNCLOS, UN, pp. 54-55.

329. Tonnesson, "History of the Dispute," p. 14.

330. Koivurova, p. 365.

331. Hong, p. 60; and Fravel, "Maritime Security in the South China Sea," p. 36.

332. Fravel, "Maritime Security in the South China Sea," pp. 36-37.

333. Hong, pp. 60-61.

334. Vidas, p. 340; and Valencia, Van Dyke, and Ludwig, p. 50.

335. "South China Sea" Map, CIA; and Greenfield, p. 35.

336. SRV, "Executive Summary," pp. 3-8, especially Figure 1; and "South China Sea" Map, CIA. The cover of the Executive Summary notes that this is only a partial submission of Vietnam's claim, and could be changed or extended.

337. China also reserves the right to change or add to its continental shelf claims. People's Republic of China, "Executive Summary," *Submission by the People's Republic of China Concerning the Outer Limits of the Continental Shelf beyond 200 Nautical Miles in Part of the East Sea*, Beijing, China: PRC, December 14, 2012, pp. 1-2, 7, available from *www.un.org/depts/los/clcs_new/submissions_files/ chn63_12/executive%20summary_EN.pdf*; and "Maritime Claims of Northeast Asia" Map, CIA.

338. Coincidentally, this arc of the EEZ runs roughly along the 2,500-m isobath line in the Paracels vicinity. "South China Sea" Map, CIA.

339. SRV, "Executive Summary," *Submission to the Commission on the Limits of the Continental Shelf*, p. 5; "Maritime Claims of Northeast Asia" Map, CIA; and "South China Sea" Map, CIA.

340. In an interesting twist, Greenfield explains an argument used by the PRC in the Spratly Islands:

> That existing precedent, which has ignored small islands on shelf delimitation between states, is confined to those cases where midway islands in fact belonged to one or other of the states between which a line was sought to be drawn in a fairly limited area of sea space. In this case, if the Spratlys belong to China (which occupies some of them), they belong to a much more distant state, but in such cases any argument that such islands should in that case have a much wider shelf claim — rather than for example constitute a territorial sea enclave — would be one equally without much established precedent or authority.

This argument seems to work against any claim that the PRC might make for the continental shelf around the Paracels that extends into Vietnamese continental baseline claims. The only exception in international law from this precedent is the 1976 Channel Islands Case, but that was not repeated in the French-Canadian St. Pierre et Micquelon solution that followed. Greenfield, p. 37.

341. Fravel, *Strong Borders, Secure Nation*, pp. 267-269; Hong, p. 73; and Dolven, Kan, and Manyin, p. 12.

342. Tonnesson, "Geopolitics and Maritime Territorial Disputes," p. 112.

343. These ASEAN states include Malaysia, the Philippines, and Brunei. Hong, p. 55; and "South China Sea," USEIA.

344. Hong, p. 19; Valencia, Van Dyke, and Ludwig, pp. 36-37; and Joyner.

345. "South China Sea," USEIA; and Amer, "Claims and Conflict Situations," p. 31.

346. Greenfield, p. 40.

347. Valencia, Van Dyke and Ludwig, p. 27; Greenfield, pp. 38-39; and "South China Sea" Map, CIA.

348. "Roiling the Waters," p. 39; and Judy Hua and Chen Aizyu, "China's CNOOC Tenders another 26 Offshore Blocks, Many in South China Sea," *Reuters,* August 28, 2012, available from *www.reuters.com/article/2012/08/28/china-cnooc-blocks-idUSL 4E8JS03R20120828.*

349. Greenfield, pp. 38-39; Van Dyke and Bennett, p. 73; Fravel, "Maritime Security in the South China Sea," p. 37; and "South China Sea" Map, CIA.

350. The Philippines has also challenged both Vietnam's continental shelf submission in the northern South China Sea and the joint Malaysia-Vietnam submission in the southern South China Sea. Indonesia protested China's protest as being too broad. "Submissions, Through the Secretary-General of the United Nations,

to the Commission on the Limits of the Continental Shelf, Pursuant to Article 76, Paragraph 8, of the UN Convention on the Law of the Sea of 10 December 1982," New York: UN Division for Ocean Affairs and the Law of the Sea, updated September 4, 2013, available from *www.un.org/depts/los/clcs_new/commission_submissions.htm.*

351. Sutter and Huang, pp. 71-72.

352. Joyner.

353. UNCLOS, UN, p. 67; and Valencia, Van Dyke, and Ludwig, p. 58.

354. Paal, "Territorial Disputes in Asian Waters."

355. Jin; and *South China Sea (II),* ICG, p. 29.

356. Shicun Wu, p. 365; Joyner; Greenfield, p. 34; and Kivimaki, Odgaard, and Tonnesson, p. 153.

357. Hong, p. 66.

358. Joyner.

359. Fravel, "Maritime Security in the South China Sea," pp. 35-36.

360. Valencia, Van Dyke, and Ludwig, p. 44; and Greenfield, p. 36.

361. Dolven, Kan, and Manyin, p. 31.

362. Ian Townsend-Gault, "Legal and Political Perspectives on Sovereignty over the Spratly Islands," Knut Snildal, ed., *Perspectives on the Conflict in the South China Sea (Workshop Proceedings),* Oslo, Norway: Center for Development and the Environment, University of Oslo, 1999, p.11.

363. O'Rourke, *China Naval Modernization,* p. 44; and Steven Metz, "Strategic Horizons: U.S. Must Change its Thinking on Conflict in Asia," *World Politics Review,* December 12, 2012, avail-

able from *www.worldpoliticsreview.com/articles/12561/strategic-hori-zons-u-s-must-change-its-thinking-on-conflict-in-asia.*

364. Dolven, Kan, and Manyin, pp. i-ii.

365. Hillary Rodham Clinton, "Remarks at Press Availability," Hanoi, Vietnam: National Convention Center, July 23, 2010, available from *www.state.gov/secretary/rm/2010/07/145095.htm*; and Lai, *The United States and China in Power Transition*, p. 140.

366. Xinbo Wu, *China and the United States: Core Interests, Common Interests, and Partnership*, Washington DC: United States Institute of Peace, June 2011, pp. 1-2; and Clinton.

367. Sutter and Huang, p. 70.

368. Kivimaki, Odgaard, and Tonnesson, p. 151.

369. Fravel, "Maritime Security in the South China Sea," p. 47; and Constance Johnson, "China/Vietnam: South China Sea Agreement," Washington, DC: The Law Library of Congress, October 11, 2011, available from *www.loc.gov/lawweb/servlet/lloc_news?disp3_l205402849_text.*

370. Kate and Lerman.

371. Paal, "Dangerous Shoals."

372. Hong, p. 84; O'Rourke, *Maritime Territorial and EEZ Disputes,* pp. 30-31; and *Maritime Security and Navigation*, Washington DC: Department of State, Bureau of Oceans and International Environment, undated, available from *www.state.gov/e/oes/ocns/opa/maritimesecurity/.*

373. Lai, *The United States and China in Power Transition*, p. 120; Fravel, "Maritime Security in the South China Sea," p. 35; "South China Sea," USEIA; and O'Rourke, *Maritime Territorial and EEZ Disputes*, p. 33.

374. Hong, p. 30; and Sutter and Huang p. 69.

375. Fravel, "Maritime Security in the South China Sea," p. 35; Shicun Wu, pp. 369-371; Xue, p. 184; O'Rouke, *China Naval Modernization,* p. 5; and Dolven, Kan, and Manyin, p. 23.

376. Kivimaki, Odgaard, and Tonnesson, pp. 139-140; and Wiencek and Baker.

377. Mahnken, p. 12.

378. Moller, p. 75; Valencia, Van Dyke, and Ludwig, pp. 100, 131; and Hong, p. 84.

379. *South China Sea (II)*, ICG, p. 24.

380. Dolven, Kan, and Manyin, p. 32. Vietnam established a new national *Law on the Sea* in July 2012, which also clarified its maritime jurisdictions, its desires to peacefully settle the disputes, and reiterated its claims over the Paracel and Spratly Islands, increasing tensions again with China. Loi Huynh, "Vietnam: New National Law Intensifies International Dispute," Washington, DC: The Law Library of Congress, July 19, 2012, available from *www.loc.gov/lawweb/servlet/lloc_news?disp3_l205403248_text*.

381. Dutton, p. 213; Bernard Moreland, "US-China Civil Maritime Operational Engagement," Andrew S. Erickson, Lyle J. Goldstein, and Nan Li, eds., *China, the United States, and 21st Century Sea Power*, Newport, RI: Naval Institute Press, 2010, p. 168; and Brown.

382. Lai, *The United States and China in Power Transition*, p. 119.

383. O'Rourke, "Maritime Territorial and EEZ Disputes," pp. 37-38.

384. Moreland, pp. 168-169; and Dutton, p. 225.

385. Zbigniew Brzezinski, "Balancing the East, Upgrading the West: U.S. Grand Strategy in an Age of Upheaval," *Foreign Affairs*, Vol. 91, No. 1, January-February 2012, p. 101; and O'Rourke, *Maritime Territorial and EEZ Disputes*, pp. 49-50.

386. Eric A. McVadon, "Humanitarian Operations: A Window to US-China Maritime Cooperation," Andrew S. Erickson, Lyle J. Goldstein, and Nan Li, eds., *China, the United States, and 21st Century Sea Power*, Newport, RI: Naval Institute Press, 2010, p. 266.

387. Jeremy Page, "China Won't Necessarily Observe New Conduct Code for Navies," *The Wall Street Journal*, April 23, 2014, available from *online.wsj.com/news/articles/SB100014240527023047 88404579519303809875852*.

388. This agreement was renewed as the *United States/Russian Federation Incidents as Sea and Dangerous Military Activities Agreement* in 1998 and is still enforced. Chief of Naval Operations, "United States/Russian Federation Incidents as Sea and Dangerous Military Activities Agreement" OPNAVINST 5711.96C, Washington, DC: Headquarters, U.S. Navy N3/N5, November 10, 2008, available from *www.fas.org/irp/doddir/navy/opnavinst/5711_96c.pdf*.

389. Lai, *The United States and China in Power Transition*, p. 122; and Sam Bateman, "Maritime Confidence and Security Building Measures in the Asian Pacific Region and the *Law of the Sea*," J. Crawford and D. R. Rothwell, eds., *The Law of the Sea in the Asia Pacific Region*, Boston, MA: Martinus Nijhoff Publishers, 1995, p. 228.

390. These previous general international agreements include the October 1972 *Convention on the International Regulations for Preventing Collisions at Sea* (COLREGS) and the Western Pacific Naval Symposium's *Code for Unalerted Encounters at Sea* (CUES) released in 2000. The MMCA lacks established communications signals to be used at sea and an annual review of the process, both of which the INCSEA included. O'Rourke, *Maritime Territorial and EEZ Disputes*, pp. 512-513; and Brown.

391. Griffiths, p. 43; and Hong, p. 89.

392. Shicun Wu, p. 371; and Jin.

393. McVadon, p. 266; Kate and Lerman; and Brown.

394. Shicun Wu, p. 372; and Huayou Zhu, "Enhancing Sino-US Maritime Security Cooperation in Southeast Asia," Andrew S. Erickson, Lyle J. Goldstein, and Nan Li, eds., *China, the United States, and 21st Century Sea Power*, Newport, RI: Naval Institute Press, 2010, p. 383.

395. Audrey McAvoy, "Chinese Ships Visit Hawaii for Exercises with U.S," *Associated Press*, September 9, 2013, available from *www.military.com/daily-news/2013/09/09/chinese-ships-visit-hawaii-for-exercises-with-us.html?comp=7000023468025&rank=1*.

396. Shicun Wu, p. 371, and Xue, p. 184.

397. Dolven, Kan, and Manyin, p. ii.

398. Dutton, p. 223; and Goldstein, p. 127.

399. Dutton, p. 223; McVadon, pp. 280-281; Fravel, "Maritime Security in the South China Sea," p. 46; and Moreland, p. 154.

400. Perlez, "Chinese, with Revamped Force," p. A9.

401. Gabriel Collins, p. 31.

402. Indeed, the U.S. Army has already jump-started the process of gaining regional expertise in a variety of other ways. Training and Doctrine Command (TRADOC) has formed the TRADOC Cultural Center (TCC), expanded operations at the Defense Language Institute Foreign Language Center (DLIFLC), and developed the University of Foreign Military and Cultural Studies (UFMCS). Proper recruitment, management, and retention of so many selected skills will be a challenge to the Institutional Army, as it may already realize through managing its Special Forces soldiers, and it will require a sustained investment in money and resources. Scott G. Wuestner, *Building Partner Capacity/Security Force Assistance: A New Structural Paradigm*," Carlisle, PA: Strategic Studies Institute, U.S. Army War College, 2009, pp. 12-13, available from *www.strategicstudiesinstitute.army.mil/pubs/display.cfm?pubID=880*; Steve Griffin, "Regionally-Aligned Brigades: There's More to This Plan Than Meets the Eye," *Small Wars Journal*, September 19, 2012, available from *smallwarsjournal.com/jrnl/art/regionally-aligned-brigades-theres-more-to-this-plan-than-meets-*

the-eye; David Vergun, "Army Partnering for Peace," U.S. Army New Service, October 25, 2012, available from *www.army.mil/ article/90010/Army_partnering_for_peace__security/*; and "Regional Alignment in Joint and Combined Exercises," *Stand To*, Washington, DC: U.S. Army, August 28, 2013, available from *www.army. mil/standto/archive_2013-08-28/?s_cid=standto*.

403. John Vandiver, "AFRICOM First to Test New Regional Brigade Concept," *Stars and Stripes*, May 17, 2012, available from *www.stripes.com/news/africom-first-to-test-new-regional-brigade-concept-1.177476*; and Vergun.

404. Otto Kreisher, "DOD Too Cautious: 'We Have to be Willing to Fail,' Says Flournoy," *AOL Defense.Com*, December 12, 2012, available from *defense.aol.com/2012/12/12/dod-too-cautious-we-have-to-be-willing-to-fail-says-flournoy*.

405. Robert M. Chamberlain, "Back to Reality: Why Land Power Trumps in the National Rebalance toward Asia," *Armed Forces Journal*, May 2013, available from *www.armedforcesjournal. com/archive/issue/2013/05/toc*; and *Foreign Military Training and DoD Engagement Activities of Interest, 2009-10*, Washington DC: U.S. Department of Defense and Department of State, 2010, Vol. I, Sec. III-I, p. 44, available from *www.state.gov/t/pm/rls/rpt/fmtrpt/*.

406. Raymond T. Odierno, *2012 Army Strategic Planning Guidance*, Washington DC: U.S. Department of the Army, April 19, 2012, p. 6, available from *usarmy.vo.llnwd.net/e2/c/downloads/243816.pdf*.

407. David J. Berteau and Michael J. Green *et al.*, *U.S. Force Posture Strategy in the Asia Pacific Region: An Independent Assessment*, Washington DC: Center for Strategic and International Studies, 2012, p. 91, available from *csis.org/files/publication/120814_FINAL_PACOM_optimized.pdf*; Michelle Tan, "Army Assigns 4-Star, 79,000 Troops to USARPAC," *Army Times*, June 4, 2013, available from *www.armytimes.com/article/20130604/NEWS/306040003/ Army-assigns-4-star-79-000-troops-USARPAC*; and Amber Robinson, "USARPAC Becomes 4-Star Headquarters during Change of Command," Washington DC: U.S. Army Public Affairs Office, July 3, 2013, available from *www.army.mil/article/106821/*.

408. U.S. Army, "Regional Alignment in Joint and Combined Exercises."

409. James Dunnigan, "If It Works for Special Forces . . ." *Strategy Page*, October 8, 2012, available from *www.strategypage.com/dls/articles/If-It-Works-For-Special-Forces...-10-8-2012.asp.*

410. "Active Component Army Civil Affairs Units," Civil Affairs Association, undated, available from *www.civilaffairsassoc.org/civilaffairsassociation/our-nations-civil-affairs-units/active-component-army-civil-affairs-units/*; and GlobalSecurity, "364th Civil Affairs Brigade (Airborne)," Alexandria, VA: *GlobalSecurity.org*, undated, available from *www.globalsecurity.org/military/agency/army/364ca-bde.htm.*

411. Michelle Tan, "1st Regionally Aligned BCT to Deploy to Africa," *Military Times*, February 20, 2013, available from *www.militarytimes.com/article/20130220/NEWS/302200333/1st-regionally-aligned-BCT-deploy-Africa*; and Vergun.

412. *State Partnership Program: Improved Oversight, Guidance, and Training Needed for National Guard's Efforts with Foreign Partners,* Washington DC: U.S. Government Accountability Office (USGAO), May 2012, pp. 9, 25, available from *www.gao.gov/assets/600/590840.pdf.*

413. Vergun; and USGAO, p. 36.

414. "Oregon National Guard, Vietnam Sign Partnership Pact," Armed Forces Press Service (AFPS), November 30, 2012, available from *www.defense.gov/News/NewsArticle.aspx?ID=118666.*

415. "Oregon National Guard Wraps Up State Partnership Program Workshop with Vietnamese Delegation," Washington DC: US Army National Guard, April 25, 2013, available from *www.nationalguard.mil/News/ArticleView/tabid/5563/Article/3928/oregon-national-guard-wraps-up-state-partnership-program-workshop-with-vietname.aspx.*

416. USGAO, pp. 2, 7-9; AFPS, "Oregon National Guard"; and U.S. Army National Guard, "Oregon National Guard Wraps Up State Partnership Program Workshop."

417. Lewis M. Stern, "U.S.-Vietnam Defense Relations: Deepening Ties, Adding Relevance," No. 246, New York: Strategic Forum, 2009, available from *usacac.army.mil/cac2/call/docs/10-51/ch_6.asp*; and John David Ciociari, *The Limits of Alignment: Southeast Asia and the Great Powers Since 1975,* Washington, DC: Georgetown University Press, 2010, p. 122.

418. Sutter and Huang, p. 70; and Pan.

419. Berteau and Green, p. 36.

420. Paul McLeary, "U.S. Unit's Africa Deployment Will Test New Regional Concept," *Defense News Online,* September 26, 2012, available from *www.defensenews.com/article/20120926/DEFREG04/309260003/U-S-Unit-8217-s-Africa-Deployment-Will-Test-New-Regional-Concept.*

421. Tan, "1st Regionally Aligned BCT."

422. McLeary.

423. Berteau and Green, pp. 91-92.

424. U.S. Navy Task Force 73 Public Affairs, "U.S. Navy Begins Fourth Annual Naval Engagement Activity with Vietnam," Fort Smith, HI: US Pacific Fleet, April 23, 2013, available from *www.pacom.mil/media/news/2013/04/23-usnavy-4th-annual-naval-engagement-with-vietnam.shtml.*

425. Margaret Hughes, "USMC Forms MCTAG; Consolidates Reconnaissance Training," *Small Wars Journal,* November 19, 2007, available from *smallwarsjournal.com/blog/usmc-forms-mctag*; and Brian Villard, "U.S. Marine Corps Security Cooperation Group: Partnering with Foreign Militaries to Enhance Global Stability and Security," *The Official Web Site of the U.S. Marine Corps,* October 3, 2011, available from *www.mcscg.marines.mil/News/NewsArticleDisplay/tabid/2925/Article/70823/us-marine-corps-security-cooperation-group-partnering-with-foreign-militaries-t.aspx.*

426. Dunnigan.

427. Stern; and Berteau and Green, p. 36.

428. Stern.

429. Berteau and Green, pp. 36-37.

430. Griffin; and Dan Cox, "An Enhanced Plan for Regionally Aligning Brigades Using Human Terrain Systems," *Small Wars Journal,* June 14, 2012, available from *smallwarsjournal.com/jrnl/art/an-enhanced-plan-for-regionally-aligning-brigades-using-human-terrain-systems.*

431. Griffin; and Wuestner, pp. 14-16, 36-37.

432. Griffin.

433. Mcleary. These phases refer to DoD's six phases of the Continuum of Military Operations. Phase 0 is "Shape the Environment," Phase 1 is "Deter the Enemy," and Phase 2 is "Seize the Initiative."

434. Berteau and Green, p. 90.

435. Wuestner, p. 30; and Vergun.

436. Vandiver.

437. Xue, p. 187.

438. Roger Rufe, "Statement of Roger Rufe, President of the Ocean Conservancy [Private]," Testimony before the Senate Committee on Foreign Relations, Washington, DC, October 21, 2003, pp. 2-3, available from *www.foreign.senate.gov/imo/media/doc/RufeTestimony031021.pdf.*

439. Dolven, Kan, and Manyin, p. 32.

440. Dolven, Kan, and Manyin, pp. ii, 5; Clinton; and Shearer, p. 200.

441. Dolven, Kan, and Manyin, p. 32; and Fravel, "Maritime Security in the South China Sea," p. 35.

442. Shearer, p. 219. One major historic maritime claim case settled by the International Court of Justice was the Gulf of Fonseca Case in 1992. This was different, however, because the surrounding geography of the Gulf of Fonseca was a minor bay between Honduras, Nicaragua, and El Salvador, and the claims stemmed from an established unified claim from the Federal Republic of Central America. After the demise of the Federal Republic in 1839, this claim was not defined among its subsequent members. This would not be a good precedent for the South China Sea, which is more open and never had a recognized unified claim. Valencia, Van Dyke, and Ludwig, p. 17.

443. Hong, pp. 70-71.

444. Valencia, Van Dyke, and Ludwig, p. 26.

445. Valencia, Van Dyke, and Ludwig, p. 25; Shearer, p. 208; and Clinton.

446. Clinton.

447. Djalal, "South China Seas Island Disputes," p. 129; *South China Sea (II)*, ICG, pp. 29-30; Swaine and Fravel, "China's Assertive Behavior—Part One: On 'Core Interests,'" p. 10; and USEIA, "South China Sea."

448. Valencia, Van Dyke, and Ludwig, p. 78.

449. Dodds, p. 14.

450. Hong, p. 67.

451. Hong, p. 63. This split of rights would be similar to the Torres Strait Treaty negotiated between Papua New Guinea and Australia in 1978. Here, the inhabitants of Australian islands in the EEZ of Papua New Guinea were given rights to fish in the area, but other rights were kept for the coastal EEZ state. Van Dyke and Bennett, p. 83.

452. Dodds, p. 14; *South China Sea (II)*, ICG, p. 4.

453. *South China Sea (II),* ICG, p. 20.

454. Paal, "Dangerous Shoals."

455. Sutter and Huang, p. 70.

456. Valencia, Van Dyke, and Ludwig, p. 78; and Paal, "Dangerous Shoals."

457. *South China Sea (II),* ICG, p. 4.

458. Valencia, Van Dyke, and Ludwig, p. 1.

459. Amer, "Ongoing Efforts in Conflict Management," p. 120; and *South China Sea (II),* ICG, p. 30.

460. Lai, *The United States and China in Power Transition,* p. 140.

461. USPACOM, p. 2.

462. O'Rourke, "Maritime Territorial and EEZ Disputes," Summary page.

463. "South China Sea," USEIA; and Fravel, "Maritime Security in the South China Sea," p. 35. Not challenging commercial transit through historic waters presents a dilemma for Chinese and Vietnamese claims. Allowing uncontrolled passage undercuts their historic claims, since historic waters should be governed as closely as internal sovereign waterways. However, to regulate free passage in one of the world's busiest waterways would unleash an international outcry and action that could eliminate any support for their current assertions and remove historic waters as a bargaining position. This is an example of why international approbation is a necessary part of the International Court of Justice's criteria for granting historic waters status. Valencia, Van Dyke, and Ludwig, p. 28.

464. UNCLOS, UN, p. 25.

465. For instance, in Article 116 "Right to Fish on the High Seas" and Articles 186 to 191 under the "Settlement of Disputes and Advisory Options" section pertaining to the Seabed Disputes

Chamber of the International Tribunal of the *Law of the Sea*. UN-CLOS, UN, pp. 65, 95-97.

466. Valencia, Van Dyke, and Ludwig, p. 146. In the same vein, Article 82 requires coastal states to also make a payment of 1 to 7 percent on the value or volume of production from the continental shelf area between 200 and 350-nm offshore, which is the extended continental shelf that reaches into otherwise international waters. UNCLOS, UN, pp. 55-56.

467. UNCLOS, UN, p. 67.

468. Valencia, Van Dyke, and Ludwig, pp. 48, 146; Chinkin, p. 249; and Xue, p. 176.

469. Studeman; and Fravel, *Strong Borders, Secure Nation,* p. 267.

470. Valencia, Van Dyke, and Ludwig, pp. 55-56.

471. "South China Sea" Map, CIA; and Valencia, Van Dyke, and Ludwig, pp. 31, 56, 264.

472. Valencia, Van Dyke, and Ludwig, p. 265.

473. Other objectionable economic provisions concerning mandatory transfer of technology and production limitations were not enforced. Shearer, p. 200; and Rufe.

474. Hong, p. 139; and Dolven, Kan, and Manyin, p. 33.

475. Three reasons account for the lack of commercial success in mining polymetallic seabed nodules, which were the target of the ISA regime. First is the high cost and technical difficulty of mounting such operations under the severe conditions of open-ocean and extreme depths. Second is the continuing relative low cost of competing land-based sources. Third is the additional cost levied by the ISA as a "tax" to pay for its administration and to distribute to states around the world. *Wikipedia*, "Manganese Nodule," *Wikipedia.org*, undated, available from *en.wikipedia.org/wiki/Manganese_nodule*.

476. Hong, p. 2.

477. Valencia, Van Dyke, and Ludwig, pp. 3, 215.

478. Kivimaki, Odgaard, and Tonnesson, p. 152; Valencia, Van Dyke, and Ludwig, pp. 183-184; and "South China Sea" Map, CIA.

479. Clinton.

480. Valencia, Van Dyke, and Ludwig, pp. 45, 56, 205.

481. Dodds, p. 14.

482. Jin; and Studeman.

483. Normally this is interpreted to mean shelving the maritime jurisdiction disputes, not those over island sovereignty. Fravel, "Maritime Security in the South China Sea," p. 45; Djalal, "South China Seas Island Disputes," p. 125; and Hong, p. 181.

484. Valencia, Van Dyke, and Ludwig, p. 97; Dolven, Kan, and Manyin, p. 26; *South China Sea (II)*, ICG, p. 7; Studeman ; and Trillanes, p. 7.

485. *South China Sea (II)*, ICG, p. 34.

486. Valencia, Van Dyke, and Ludwig, p. 101.

487. Hong, p. 73; and Dolven, Kan, and Manyin, p. 12.

488. Boudreau, "China Vietnam Expand Joint Exploration Deal."

489. Fravel, "Maritime Security in the South China Sea," p. 46.

490. Sutter and Huang, p. 69.

491. Transnational ecotourism initiatives have had some intra-ASEAN success in the form of the Brunei-Indonesia-Malaysia-Philippines East ASEAN Growth Area (BIMP-EAGA) through government and private sector investment, which could include the Spratly Islands. Kivimaki, "Conclusion," p. 168.

492. Hasjim Djalal, *Preventive Diplomacy in Southeast Asia: Lessons Learned,* Jakarta, Indonesia: The Habibie Center, 2002, p. 79.

493. *South China Sea (II),* ICG, p. 6; and Hong, p. 185.

494. Boudreau, "China Vietnam Expand Joint Exploration Deal."

495. Chan and Li, p. 7; and Wong.

496. David M. Ong, "The 1979 and 1990 Malaysia-Thailand Joint Development Agreements: A Model for International Legal Co-operation in Common Offshore Petroleum Deposits?" *The International Journal of Marine and Coastal Law,* Vol. 14, No. 2, 1999, p. 213, Tonnesson, "Geopolitics and Maritime Territorial Disputes," pp. 112-113; and Djalal, "South China Sea Island Disputes," p. 116.

497. Tonnesson, "Geopolitics and Maritime Territorial Disputes," pp. 112-113; and Odgaard, p. 32.

498. Dolven, Kan, and Manyin, p. 30; Clinton; and Hong, p. 14.

499. Chamberlain.

500. Clinton.

501. Kreisher.

502. Dolven, Kan, and Manyin, pp. i-ii.

503. Hong, p. 197.

504. Brzezinski, p. 97.

505. Chamberlain.

506. Jianzhong Zhuang, "China's Maritime Development and US-China Cooperation," Andrew S. Erickson, Lyle J. Goldstein, and Nan Li, eds., *China, the United States, and 21st Century Sea*

Power, Newport, RI: Naval Institute Press, 2010, p. 8; Lai, *The United States and China in Power Transition,* p. 198; Fravel, *Strong Borders, Secure Nation,* p. 1; and Sanderson.

507. People's Republic of China, "China, U.S. Pledge to Build Constructive Strategic Partnership," Washington, DC: Embassy of the People's Republic of China, April 1999, available from *www. china-embassy.org/eng/zmgx/zysj/zrjfm/t36212.htm;* Randy Forbes, "China. There, I Said It," *PacNet,* Vol. 34, Pacific Forum CSIS, June 5, 2012, p. 1, available from *www.pacforum.org;* and Erikson and Goldstein, p. xi.

508. Odgaard, p. 33. Since 1949, China has been involved in 23 territorial disputes in which it has negotiated settlements to 17, sometimes offering substantial compromises. China's motivation for land concessions in territorial disputes may be to manage internal ethnic unrest in those areas in order to better govern its dominions. In disputes involving its designated core homeland, like Tibet or Taiwan, and in island disputes China has been much less accommodating. This leads some to question China's commitment to coexistence, especially concerning "national identity issues." Odgaard, pp. 31-34; and Fravel, *Strong Borders, Secure Nation,* pp. 1-2, 6.

509. Sutter and Huang, p. 67; and Ciociari, p. 127.

510. Amer, "Ongoing Efforts in Conflict Management," pp. 119-120.

511. Fravel, "Maritime Security in the South China Sea," p. 47; and Ciociari, p. 131.

512. *National Security Presidential Directive 41, Maritime Security Policy,* Washington DC: The White House, December 21, 2004, available from *www.fas.org/irp/offdocs/nspd/nspd41.pdf;* and Dutton, p. 197.

513. USPACOM, pp. 3-5.

514. Clinton.

515. Andrew S. Erickson, "Chinese Views of America's New Maritime Strategy," Andrew S. Erickson, Lyle J. Goldstein, and

Nan Li, eds., *China, the United States, and 21st Century Sea Power*, Newport, RI: Naval Institute Press, 2010, p. 431.

516. Valencia, Van Dyke, and Ludwig, p. 5; and Hong, p. 198.

517. Wiencek and Baker; Moller, p. 75; Amer, "Ongoing Efforts in Conflict Management," p. 123; and Kivimaki, Odgaard, and Tonnesson, p. 146.

518. Valencia, Van Dyke, and Ludwig, p. 111.

519. Kivimaki, Odgaard, and Tonnesson, p. 143; Wiencek and Baker; Spitzer; Erickson, p. 431; Xinbo Wu, *US Security Policy in Asia: Implications for China-US Relations*, Washington DC: The Brookings Institution, September 2000, available from *www.brookings.edu/research/papers/2000/09/northeastasia-xinbo*; Kate and Lerman; and Dutton, p. 208.

520. Wiencek and Baker; Chan and Li, p. 9; and Perlez, "China and Vietnam Point Fingers."

521. Wu, *US Security Policy in Asia: Implications for China-US Relations*; Fravel, "Maritime Security in the South China Sea," p. 34.

522. Kivimaki, Odgaard, and Tonnesson, pp. 139-140; Shicun Wu, pp. 368-369; Forbes, p. 1; and Wu, *US Security Policy in Asia: Implications for China-US Relations*. Following the Mischief Reef incident:

> on 16 June 1995 . . . Joseph Nye, then US Assistant Secretary of Defense for International Security, said, 'if military action occurred in the Spratlys and this interfered with the freedom of the seas, then we would be prepared to escort and make sure that navigation continues.' This was the first time that a US high-level official expressed the possibility of US military intervention on the SCS [South China Sea] issue on the basis of its interference with navigation (Shicun Wu, p. 369).

523. Lai, *The United States and China in Power Transition*, pp. 137, 143.

524. Kevin Rudd, "A New Road Map for U.S-Chinese Relations," *Foreign Affairs*, Vol. 92, No. 2, March/April 2013, pp. 12-13.

525. Lai, *The United States and China in Power Transition*, p. 137; Hong, p. 196; and Kivimaki, Odgaard, and Tonnesson, pp. 142-143, 147.

526. Other regional access includes Thailand's U Tapao, Malaysia's Lamut, and Indonesia's Surabaya, and basing rights at Singapore's Changi Naval Base and the Philippines' former-U.S. naval base at Subic Bay. Moller, p. 76; Hong, p. 198; Gopal Ratman, "Cam Ranh Bay Lures Panetta Seeking Return to Vietnam Port," *Bloomberg News*, June 4, 2012, available from *www.bloomberg.com/news/2012-06-04/cam-ranh-bay-lures-panetta-seeking-u-s-return-to-vietnam-port.html*; Michael Cohen, "Philippines, U.S. Confirm US Navy's Return to Subic Bay," *IHS Jane's Defence Weekly*, October 10, 2012, available from *www.janes.com/article/13538/philippines-us-confirm-us-navy-s-return-to-subic-bay*; and Jamie Laude, "US Troops Can Use Clark, Subic Bases," *The Philippine Star*, June 6, 2012, available from *www.ajdigitaledition.com/pdfs/PDF/2012_LA/2012_06_09/2012_LA_06_09_A%2014.pdf*. Treaty allies offer basing rights in Japan, South Korea, and Australia at Darwin, and support for a continued strong U.S. presence in the Asia-Pacific region. Robson.

527. Such conflict includes PRC involvement in the Korean War, the shelling of the Taiwanese-occupied offshore islands of Quemoy in 1958, the PRC's brief war with India in 1962, the border skirmishes with the Soviet Union in 1969, and the PRC invasion of Vietnam in 1979. Fravel attributes this behavior in part to concerns with its own weakness, as China has used force either in disputes with its militarily most powerful neighbors or in conflicts where it has occupied little or none of the land that it has claimed. Kivimaki, Odgaard, and Tonnesson, p. 144; and Fravel, *Strong Borders, Secure Nation*, pp. 2, 7, 272.

528. Controversy from remarks made by mid-level Chinese officials in 2010 have left it uncertain if one of the PRC's declared core interests of sovereignty over China's territory, which it considers non-negotiable, also includes the South China Sea islands. If indeed that was not the intent of the Chinese government, some believe that China's interests are nonetheless moving in that di-

rection. Swaine and Fravel, "China's Assertive Behavior—Part One: On 'Core Interests,'" p. 2; Fravel, "Maritime Security in the South China Sea," p. 42; Dueck; and Jisi Wang, "China's Search for a Grand Strategy: A Rising Great Power Finds Its Way," *Foreign Affairs*, Vol. 90, No. 2, March-April 2011, pp. 70-71.

529. Kivimaki, Odgaard, and Tonnesson, pp. 134-135; and Moller, p. 76.

530. In 2010, President Obama cancelled two Asian trips due to domestic crises over passing healthcare reform and the Gulf of Mexico oil spill, and in 2013 cancelled attendance at both the Asia-Pacific Economic Cooperation and the East Asia Summit conferences in Southeast Asia over the government shutdown crisis, conceding the diplomatic initiative to China and leaving some analysts wondering how much the United States is committed to the region and the extent of its leadership in the world.

531. "Roiling the Waters."

532. Hong, p. 196; Boudreau, "Vietnam Leader in China Seeks Export Gains Amid Sea Tension"; Kivimaki, Odgaard, and Tonnesson, p. 142; and *South China Sea (II)*, ICG, p. 26.

533. Dueck; and Mahnken, pp. 1, 14.

534. O'Rourke, "Maritime Territorial and EEZ Disputes," pp. 16-19.

535. *South China Sea (II)*, ICG, p. 32; Kivimaki, Odgaard, and Tonnesson, p. 139; and Hong, p. 196.

536. USPACOM, pp. 2-3.

537. Chan and Li, p. 1; Sutter and Huang, p. 67; and *South China Sea (II)*, ICG, p. 23.

538. Brzezinski, pp. 99-100.

539. Dueck; Forbes, p. 1; and Kaplan, "Future of Conflict," pp. 82-83.

540. *South China Sea (II)*, ICG, pp. 23-25; and Paal, "Dangerous Shoals."

541. These myriad activities include the frequent presence of U.S. naval ships in the region; the expansion of military bases on the U.S. island territory of Guam; naval exercises with Vietnam, including the USS *George Washington* aircraft carrier; a tripling of port calls to Malaysia over 10 years; and an agreement for much needed enhanced bilateral security cooperation with the Philippines, such as a land-based radar to track ships and *Hamilton* class cutters. Kivimaki, Odgaard, and Tonnesson, pp. 141-142; Shicun Wu, p. 370; Wu, *US Security Policy in Asia: Implications for China-US Relations*; Pan; Hong pp. 28, 30, 196-198; *South China Sea (II)*, ICG, pp. 11, 26; Sutter and Huang, p. 70; and Dolven, Kan, and Manyin, p. 29.

542. Mahnken, pp. 1, 4.

543. Pan.

544. Paal, "Dangerous Shoals."

545. Sutter and Huang, p. 69.

546. Shicun Wu, p. 370; and Lai, *The United States and China in Power Transition*, p. 140.

547. Kivimaki, Odgaard, and Tonnesson, p. 147; and Valencia, Van Dyke, and Ludwig, p. 92.

548. Kivimaki, Odgaard, and Tonnesson, p. 141.

549. *Ibid.*, pp. 135, 147; and Fravel, *Strong Borders, Secure Nation*, p. 5.

550. *South China Sea (II)*, ICG, p. 25.

551. Dolven, Kan, and Manyin, p. 23.

552. Ciorciari, p. 124; and Valencia, Van Dyke, and Ludwig, p. 131.

553. Kaplan, "Future of Conflict," p. 82.

554. Hong, p. 30.

555. *South China Sea (II)*, ICG, p. 27.

556. Sutter and Huang, p. 70.

557. *Ibid.*, p. 67; and Ciorciari, p. 127.

558. Valencia, Van Dyke, and Ludwig, p. 99.

559. Odgaard, p. 20.

560. Brzezinski, p. 97.